Tequila of Life
Inspirational Tales

Tequila of Life
Inspirational Tales

Compiled & Edited by

Sharad Gupta

ALLIED PUBLISHERS PVT. LTD.
New Delhi • Mumbai • Kolkata • Lucknow • Chennai
Nagpur • Bangalore • Hyderabad • Ahmedabad

ALLIED PUBLISHERS PRIVATE LIMITED

Regd. Off.: 15 J.N. Heredia Marg, Ballard Estate, **Mumbai**–400001
Ph.: 022-22626476 • E-mail: mumbai.books@alliedpublishers.com

1/13-14 Asaf Ali Road, **New Delhi**–110002
Ph.: 011-23239001 • E-mail: delhi.books@alliedpublishers.com

17 Chittaranjan Avenue, **Kolkata**–700072
Ph.: 033-22129318 • E-mail: cal.books@alliedpublishers.com

751 Anna Salai, **Chennai**–600002
Ph.: 044-28523938 • E-mail: chennai.books@alliedpublishers.com

5th Main Road, Gandhinagar, **Bangalore**–560009
Ph.: 080-22262081 • E-mail: bngl.books@alliedpublishers.com

3-2-844/6 & 7 Kachiguda Station Road, **Hyderabad**–500027
Ph.: 040-24619079 • E-mail: hyd.books@alliedpublishers.com

60 Shiv Sunder Apartments (Ground Floor), Central Bazar Road,
Bajaj Nagar, **Nagpur**–440010

F-1 Sun House (First Floor), C.G. Road, Navrangpura,
Ellisbridge P.O., **Ahmedabad**–380006
Ph.: 079-26465916 • E-mail: ahmbd.books@alliedpublishers.com

Khasra No. 168, Plot No. 12-A, Opp. Wisdom Academy School,
Kamta, Surendra Nagar, **Lucknow**–227105
Ph.: 09335202549 • E-mail: lko.books@alliedpublishers.com

Website: www.alliedpublishers.com

© 2015, Sharad Gupta

No part of the material protected by this copyright notice may be reproduced or utilized in any form or by any means, electronic or mechanical including photocopying, recording or by any information storage and retrieval system, without prior written permission from the copyright owner.

ISBN: 978-81-8424-963-7

Published by Sunil Sachdev and printed by Ravi Sachdev at
Allied Publishers Pvt. Ltd. (Printing Division),
A-104 Mayapuri Phase II, New Delhi-110064

Preface

What a wonderful saying—when life gives you lemons, ask for tequila and salt. As tequila is bound to give us a certain high, in the same way this book promises to make us feel on top of the world and to take us to a higher level of consciousness.

In the sea of life, this book will help us to discover several islands of euphoria helping us to experience intense feelings of well-being, elation, happiness, excitement and joy.

Words that enlighten the soul are more precious than jewels. In these days of WhatsApp, E-mails and other sources of connectivity, a lot of good material comes as forwards, which one wants to share. Tequila of Life is the result of this desire. Permission of individual authors is implicit out of their magnanimity.

Richa means the writing of the Vedas. It also means a magical invocation. Richa is very special to our family as by the time you go through this preface, she would be married to my son Shashank. This book is the outcome of the immense joy I am experiencing, which I want to share with you. Please bless them and pray for their blissful happy married life.

Have a great day and be good to yourself. You deserve it!

Contents

1. Cracked Pot 11
2. Friendship 12
3. Right Perspective 14
4. I Know who She is 15
5. The Tea Cup 16
6. Story of Appreciation 18
7. What Kind of Day shall I Have 21
8. When You Thought I wasn't Looking 22
9. The Story of Ankit Gupta, MD 23
10. Ageing is Blissful 26
11. Interview with God 27
12. A New Lease of Life 29
13. The Second Chance 31
14. Humanity 33
15. I've Learned 35
16. How much does a Teacher Make 37
17. The Mirror's Fault 39
18. Lunch with God 40
19. Who can Understand Love 41
20. Happy Improvement... 42
21. Don't Hope, Decide! 45
22. Do You Build Bridges or Fences 47
23. Love Her 49
24. Things God won't Ask on that Day 50

25.	Date with a Woman ...	51
26.	Moment	53
27.	Don't Take Them for Granted	55
28.	Man with Four Wives	56
29.	Friend	58
30.	My Favourite Philosophy	59
31.	Worth it	60
32.	True Love	61
33.	Value what is Yours	64
34.	Let it be	65
35.	God's Wings	66
36.	Not as Happy as You	67
37.	Anger is Danger	68
38.	Salted Cofee	69
39.	Be a Lake	71
40.	Let's Change Our Vision	72
41.	Why do We Shout when We are Angry	73
42.	Address of God	74
43.	Hindering Growth	75
44.	The Three Trees	76
45.	Self-Improvement	79
46.	The Fresh Fish	81
47.	Prayer	82
48.	The Returned Gift	83
49.	Perfect Action	84
50.	Two Stories	85
51.	How to Stay Young	88

52.	A Tale of Two Seas	89
53.	Dirty Laundry	91
54.	Fifteen Things to Give Up	92
55.	Team Work	95
56.	Shoe Maker	96
57.	Advice to 50+ Years Old	97
58.	Perfection	99
59.	Courtesies	100
60.	Acceptance	102
61.	Making a Difference	104
62.	Start Over	105
63.	The Seed Story	106
64.	Plant with Care	108
65.	Seasons	109
66.	Follow Your Dream	110
67.	The Right Solution	111
68.	Making of a Woman	113
69.	Limitations	114
70.	Choices	115
71.	Sharpen Your Skills	117
72.	The Knots Prayer	118
73.	No Rush	119
74.	Be Thankful	120
75.	Little Things	121
76.	Perceptions	122
77.	Woman	124
78.	Situation Vacant	125

79. Now, Instead 126
80. God has Fallen in Love with You 127
81. A Special Request 128
82. Food for Thought 129
83. Christmas Present 130
84. The Rope 132
85. Don't Dance so Fast 134
86. Conditioned Minds 136
87. The Great Train Journey 137
88. What is Mine 139
89. Old Age Home 140
90. Who is Happy 141
91. The Two Falcons 142
92. If God should Go on Strike 143
93. Daughter 144

Cracked Pot

A water bearer had two large pots, each hung on the ends of a pole which he carried across his neck. One of the pots had a crack in it, while the other pot was perfect and always delivered a full portion of water. At the end of the long walk from the stream to the house, the cracked pot arrived only half full.

For a full two years this went on daily, with the bearer delivering only one and a half pots full of water to his house. Of course, the perfect pot was proud of its accomplishments, but the poor cracked pot was ashamed of its own imperfection, and miserable that it was able to accomplish only half of what it had been made to do. After two years of what it perceived to be a bitter failure, it spoke to the water bearer one day by the stream, "I am ashamed of myself, because this crack in my side causes water to leak out all the way back to your house."

The bearer said to the pot, "Did you notice that there were flowers only on your side of the path, but not on the other pot's side? That's because I have always known about your flaw, and I planted flower seeds on your side of the path, and every day while we walk back, you've watered them. I have been able to pick these beautiful flowers to decorate the table. Without you being just the way you are, there would not be this beauty to grace the house."

Moral: Each of us has our own unique flaws. We're all cracked pots. But it's the cracks and flaws we each have that make our lives together so very interesting and rewarding.

Nothing is permanent in this world, not even our troubles.

Friendship

A man and his dog were walking along a road. The man was enjoying the scenery, when it suddenly occurred to him that he was dead. He remembered dying, and that the dog walking beside him had been dead for years. He wondered where the road was leading them.

After a while, they came to a high white stone wall along one side of the road. It looked like fine marble. There was a tall arch that glowed in the sunlight. When he was standing before it he saw a magnificent gate in the arch that looked like mother-of-pearl, and the street that led to the gate looked like pure gold. He and the dog walked toward the gate, and as he got closer, he saw a man at a desk on one side. When he was close enough, he called out, "Excuse me, where are we?"

"This is Heaven, sir," the man answered.

"Wow! Would you happen to have some water?" The man asked.

"Of course, sir. Come right in, and I'll have some cold water brought right up." The man gestured, and the gate began to open.

"Can my friend," gesturing toward his dog, "come in, too?" The traveler asked.

"I'm sorry, sir, but we don't accept pets."

The man thought for a moment and then turned back toward the road and continued the way he had been going with his dog. After another long walk, and at the top of another long hill, he came to a dirt road leading through a farm gate that looked as if it had never been closed. There was no fence.

As he approached the gate, he saw a man inside, leaning against a tree and reading a book.

"Excuse me!" He asked the man. "Do you have any water?"

"Yeah, sure, there's a pump over there, come on in."

"How about my friend here?" The traveler gestured to the dog.

"There should be a bowl by the pump."

They went through the gate, and sure enough, there was an old-fashioned hand pump with a bowl beside it. The traveler took a long drink himself, and then he filled the water bowl and gave to the dog. When they were full, he and the dog walked back toward the man who was standing by the tree.

"What do you call this place?" The traveler asked.

"This is Heaven," he answered.

"Well, that's confusing," the traveler said. "The man down the road said that was Heaven, too."

"Oh, you mean the place with the gold street and pearly gates? Nope. That's hell."

"Doesn't it make you mad for them to use your name like that?"

"No, we're just happy that they screen out the folks who would leave their best friends behind."

Friends are angels who lift us to our feet when our wings have trouble remembering how to fly.

Right Perspective

The train had started moving. It was packed with people of all ages. An old man was seated with his 30 year old son near the window. As the train moved by, the son was overwhelmed with joy as he was thrilled with the scenery outside. "See dad, the scenery of green trees moving away is very beautiful."

This behaviour from a thirty year old person made other people feel strange about him. Everyone started murmuring something or other about him. "This guy seems to be mad," newly married Raj whispered to his wife.

Suddenly it started raining. Rain drops fell on the travelers through the open window. The thirty year old son, filled with joy, exclaimed "See dad, how beautiful the rain is."

Raj's wife got irritated with the rain drops spoiling her new suit. Raj snubbed, "Can't you see it is raining, you old man. If your son is not feeling well, get him soon to a mental asylum. And don't disturb public hence forth."

The old man hesitated first and then in a low tone replied "We are on the way back from hospital. My son got discharged today morning. He was blind by birth. Last week only he got his vision. The rain and nature are new to his eyes. Please forgive us for the inconvenience caused."

A blind person asked God: "Can there be anything worse than losing eye sight?"

God replied: "Yes, losing your vision!"

I Know who She is

It was a busy morning, about 8:30, when an elderly gentleman in his 80's arrived to have his stitches removed from his thumb. He said he was in a hurry as he had an appointment at 9:00 am. I saw him looking at his watch and decided that I would evaluate his wound out of turn. On examination, I found it was well healed, so I talked to one of the doctors, got the needed supplies to remove his sutures and redress his wound.

While taking care of his wound, I asked him if he had another doctor's appointment this morning, as he was in such a hurry. The gentleman told me no, that he needed to go to the nursing home to eat breakfast with his wife. I inquired about her health. He told me that she had been there for a while and that she was a victim of Alzheimer's disease. As we talked, I asked if she would be upset if he was a bit late. He replied that she no longer knew who he was, that she had not recognized him for five years now. I was surprised, and asked him, "And you still go every morning, even though she doesn't know who you are?"

He smiled as he patted my hand and said, "She doesn't know me, but I still know who she is."

The bird asked the bumblebee: "You work so hard to make the honey and humans just take it away, doesn't it make you feel bad?"

"No," said the Bee, "Because they will never take from me the art of making it."

The Tea Cup

There was a couple who liked antiques and pottery and especially teacups. One day in a shop they saw a beautiful teacup. They said, "May we see that? We've never seen one quite so beautiful."

As the lady handed it to them, suddenly the teacup spoke, "I haven't always been a teacup. There was a time when I was common clay. My master took me and rolled me and patted me over and over and I yelled out, 'Let me alone', but he only smiled, 'Not yet'."

"Then I was placed on a spinning wheel," the teacup said, "and suddenly I was spun round and round and round. 'Stop it! I'm getting dizzy!' I screamed. But the master only nodded and said, 'Not yet'."

"Then he put me in the oven. I had never felt such heat. I wondered why he wanted to burn me, and I yelled and knocked at the door. I could see him through the opening and I could read his lips as he shook his head, 'Not yet'."

"Finally the door opened, he put me on the shelf, and I began to cool. 'That's better,' I said. And he brushed and painted me all over. The fumes were horrible. I thought I would gag. 'Stop it, stop it!' I cried. He only nodded, 'Not yet'."

"Then suddenly he put me back into the oven, not like the first one. This was twice as hot and I knew I would suffocate. I begged, I pleaded, I screamed, I cried. All the time I could see him through the opening nodding his head saying, 'Not yet'."

"Then I knew there wasn't any hope. I would never make it. I was ready to give up. But the door opened and he took me out and placed me on the shelf. One hour later he handed me a mirror and said, 'Look at yourself.' And I did. I said, 'That's not me; that couldn't be me. It's beautiful. I'm beautiful'."

"I want you to remember," he said, "I know it hurts to be rolled and patted, but if I had left you alone, you'd have dried up. I know it made you dizzy to spin around on the wheel, but if I had stopped, you would have crumbled."

"I knew it hurt and was hot and disagreeable in the oven, but if I hadn't put you there, you would have cracked. I know the fumes were bad when I brushed and painted you all over, but if I hadn't done that, you never would have hardened; you would not have had any color in your life."

"And if I hadn't put you back in that second oven, you wouldn't survive for very long because the hardness would not have held. Now you are a finished product. You are what I had in mind when I first began with you."

God knows what He's doing (for all of us). He is the Potter, and we are His clay. He will mold us and make us, so that we may be made into a flawless piece of work.

Different Faces of Bhakti

When bhakti enters food it becomes prasad.

When bhakti enters water it becomes charanamrit.

When bhakti enters travel it becomes pilgrimage.

When bhakti enters music it becomes kirtan.

When bhakti enters a house it becomes a temple.

When bhakti enters actions it becomes seva.

Story of Appreciation

One young academically excellent person went to apply for a managerial position in a big company. He passed the initial rounds. The director took the final interview and discovered from the CV that the youth's academic achievements were excellent all the way, from the secondary school until the postgraduate research, never had a year when he did not score.

The director asked, "Did you obtain any scholarships in school?"

The youth answered "none".

The director asked, "Was it your father who paid for your school fees?"

The youth replied, "My father passed away when I was one year old, it was my mother who paid for my school fees."

The director asked, "Where did your mother work?"

The youth answered, "My mother worked as clothes cleaner."

The director requested the youth to show his hands. The youth showed a pair of hands that were smooth and perfect.

The director asked, "Have you ever helped your mother wash the clothes?"

The youth answered, "Never, my mother always wanted me to study and read more books. Furthermore, my mother can wash clothes faster than me."

The director said, "I have a request. When you go back today, go and clean your mother's hands, and then see me tomorrow morning."

The youth felt that his chance of landing the job was high. When he went back, he happily requested his mother to let him clean her hands. His mother felt strange as well as happy, but with mixed feelings, she showed her hands to her son.

The youth cleaned his mother's hands slowly. His tears fell as he did that. It was the first time he noticed that his mother's hands were so wrinkled, and there were so many bruises in her hands. Some bruises were so painful that his mother shivered when they were cleaned with water.

This was the first time the youth realized that it was this pair of hands that washed clothes everyday to enable him to pay the school fee. The bruises in the mother's hands were the price that the mother had to pay for his graduation, academic excellence and his future.

After finishing the cleaning of his mother's hands, the youth quietly washed all the remaining clothes for his mother. That night, mother and son talked for a very long time.

Next morning, the youth went to the director's office. The Director noticed the tears in the youth's eyes. He asked: "Can you tell me what have you done and learned yesterday in your house?"

The youth answered, "I cleaned my mother's hands, and also finished cleaning all the remaining clothes."

The Director asked, "Please tell me your feelings."

The youth said,

Number 1,

I know now what appreciation means. Without my mother, I would not be successful today.

Number 2,

By working together and helping my mother, I now realize how difficult and tough it is to get something done.

Number 3,

I have come to appreciate the importance and value of family relationship.

The director said, "This is what I am looking for to be in my manager. I want to recruit a person who can appreciate the help of others, a person who knows the sufferings of others to get things done, and a person who would not put money as his only goal in life. You are hired."

> *One night a man came to our house and told me, "There is a family with eight children. They have not eaten for days," I took some food and went to meet the family, I saw the faces of those little children disfigured by hunger. There was no sorrow or sadness in their faces, just the deep pain of hunger. I gave the food to the mother. She divided it in two, and went out, carrying half the food with her. When she came back, I asked her, "Where did you go?" She gave me this simple reply, "To my neighbours—they are hungry too."*

What Kind of Day shall I Have

I woke up early today, excited over all I get to do before the day ends.

I have responsibilities to fulfill today. I am important.

My job is to choose what kind of day I am going to have.

Today I can complain because the weather is rainy or ...
I can be thankful that the grass is getting watered for free.

Today I can grumble about my health or ...
I can rejoice that I am alive.

Today I can mourn my lack of friends or ...
I can excitedly embark upon a quest to discover new relationships.

Today I can whine because I have to go to work or ...
I can shout with joy because I have a job to do.

Today I can murmur dejectedly because I have to do housework or ...
I can feel honored because life has provided shelter for my mind, body and soul.

Today stretches ahead of me, waiting to be shaped.

And here I am, the sculptor who gets to do the shaping.

What today will be like is up to me.

I get to choose what kind of day I will have.

Why not have a Great Day!

When You Thought I wasn't Looking

When you thought I wasn't looking, I saw you hang my first painting on the refrigerator, and I immediately wanted to paint another one.

When you thought I wasn't looking, I saw you feed a stray cat, and I learned that it was good to be kind to animals.

When you thought I wasn't looking, I heard you say a prayer, and I knew that there is a God I could always talk to, and I learned to trust Him.

When you thought I wasn't looking, I saw you make a meal and take it to a friend who was sick, and I learned that we all have to take care of each other.

When you thought I wasn't looking, I saw you give your time and money to help people who had nothing, and I learned that those who have something should give to those who don't.

When you thought I wasn't looking, I saw you take care of our house and everyone in it, and I learned we have to take care of what we are given.

When you thought I wasn't looking, I learned most of life's lessons that I need to know to be a good and productive person when I grow up.

When you thought I wasn't looking, I looked at you and wanted to say, "Thanks for all the things I saw when you thought I wasn't looking."

You are not fully dressed ...

If you do not smile.

The Story of Ankit Gupta, MD

As she stood in front of her primary class V on the very first day of school, she told the children an untruth. Like most teachers, she looked at her pupils and said that she loved them all the same. However, that was impossible, because there in the front row, slumped in his seat, was a little boy named Ankit.

Mrs. Kapur had watched Ankit the year before and noticed that he did not mix well with other children, that his clothes were messy and that he constantly needed a bath. In addition, Ankit could be unpleasant. It got to the point where Mrs. Kapur would actually take delight in marking his papers with a broad red pen, making bold X's and then putting a big "F" at the top of his papers.

At the school where Mrs. Kapur taught, she was required to review each child's past records and she put Ankit's off until last. However, when she reviewed his file, she was in for a surprise.

Ankit's class I teacher had written, "Ankit is a bright child with a ready laugh. He does his work neatly and has good manners. He is a joy to be around."

His class II teacher wrote, "Ankit is an excellent pupil, well liked by his classmates, but he is troubled because his mother has a terminal illness and life at home must be a struggle."

His class III teacher wrote, "His mother's death has been hard on him. He tries to do his best, but his father doesn't show much interest and his home life will soon affect him if some steps aren't taken."

Ankit's class IV teacher wrote, "Ankit is withdrawn and doesn't show much interest in school. He doesn't have many friends and he sometimes sleeps in class."

By now, Mrs. Kapur realized the problem and she was ashamed of herself. She felt even worse when her pupils brought her teacher's day presents, wrapped in beautiful ribbons and bright paper, except for Ankit's. His present was clumsily wrapped in a heavy, brown paper that he got from a grocery bag.

Mrs. Kapur took pains to open it in the middle of other presents. Some of the children started to laugh when they saw a bracelet with some of the stones missing, and a bottle that was one-quarter full of perfume. But she stifled the children's laughter when she exclaimed how pretty the bracelet was, putting it on, and dabbing some of the perfume on her wrist.

Ankit stayed after school that day, just long enough to say, "Mrs. Kapur, today you smelled just like my Mom used to." After the children left, she cried for at least an hour. Mrs. Kapur started paying special attention to Ankit. As she worked with him, his mind seemed to come alive. More she encouraged him, faster he responded. By the end of the year, Ankit had become one of the smartest children in the class and, despite her lie that she would love all the children the same, Ankit became one of her 'pets'.

A year later, she found a note under her door, from Ankit, telling her that she was still the best teacher he ever had in his whole life.

Six years went by before she got another note from Ankit. He then wrote that he had finished secondary school, has stood first in his class, and she was still the best teacher he ever had in his whole life.

Four years after that, she got another letter, saying that he would soon graduate from the university with the highest of honors. He assured Mrs. Kapur that she was still the best and favorite teacher he had ever had in his whole life.

Four more years passed and yet another letter came. This time he explained that after he got his bachelor's degree, he decided to go a little further. The letter explained that she was still the best and favorite teacher he ever had. But now his name was a little longer. The letter was signed, Ankit Gupta, MD.

The story does not end here. You see, there was yet another letter that spring. Ankit said he had met this girl and was going to be married. He explained that his father had died a couple of years ago and he was wondering if Mrs. Kapur might agree to sit at the wedding in the place that was usually reserved for the mother of the groom.

Of course, Mrs. Kapur did. And guess what? She wore the same bracelet, the one with several stones missing. Moreover, she made sure she was wearing the same perfume that Ankit remembered his mother wearing. They hugged each other, and Dr. Ankit whispered in Mrs. Kapur's ear, "Thank you Mrs. Kapur for believing in me. Thank you so much for making me feel important and showing me that I could make a difference."

Mrs. Kapur, with tears in her eyes, whispered back. She said, "Ankit, you have it all wrong. You were the one who taught me that I could make a difference. I didn't know how to teach until I met you."

> *When you pray for others, God listens to you and blesses them, and sometimes, when you are safe and happy, remember that someone has prayed for you.*

Ageing is Blissful

As I've aged, I've become kinder to myself, and less critical of myself. I've become my own friend. I have finally understood the great freedom that comes with aging.

Whose business is it if I choose to read or play on the computer until 4 am or sleep until noon. I will dance with myself to those wonderful tunes of the 60s & 70s, and if I, at the same time, wish to weep over a lost love, I will. I will walk the beach in a swim suit that is stretched over a bulging body, and will dive into the waves with abandon if I choose to, despite the pitying glances from the jet set.

Sure, over the years my heart has been broken. How can your heart not break when you lose a loved one, or when a child suffers. But broken hearts are what give us strength, understanding and compassion. A heart never broken will never know the joy of being imperfect.

I am so blessed to have lived long enough to have my hair turning grey, and to have my youthful laughs be forever etched into deep grooves on my face. So many have never laughed, and so many have died before their hair could turn silver.

As you get older, it is easier to be positive. You care less about what other people think. I don't question myself anymore. I've even earned the right to be wrong.

I like being old. It has set me free. I like the person I have become. I am not going to live forever, but while I am still here, I will not waste time lamenting what could have been, or worrying about what will be. I will simply live!

Interview with God

I dreamed I had an interview with God.

"So you would like to interview me?" God asked.

"If you have the time." I said.

God smiled "My time is eternity. What questions do you have in mind for me?"

"What surprises you most about humankind?"

God answered, "That they get bored with childhood. They rush to grow up and then long to be children again."

"That they lose their health to make money and then lose their money to restore their health."

"That by thinking anxiously about the future, they forget the present, such that they live in neither the present nor the future."

"That they live as if they will never die, and die as if they had never lived."

God's hand took mine and we were silent for a while. Then I asked, "As a parent, what are some of life's lessons you want your children to learn?"

God replied with a smile, "To learn they cannot make anyone love them. What they can do is let themselves love somebody."

"To learn that it is not good to compare themselves to others."

"To learn that a rich person is not one who has the most, but is one who needs the least."

"To learn that it only takes a few seconds to open wounds in persons we love, and it takes many years to heal them."

"To learn to forgive by practicing forgiveness."

"To learn that there are persons who love them dearly, but simply do not know how to express or show their feelings."

"To learn that two people can look at the same thing and see it differently."

"To learn that it is not always enough that they be forgiven by others but that they must forgive themselves."

"And to learn that I am always there."

Best Exercise.... is Walking....

A lot of 'walking away' will do your life good.

'Walk away' from arguments that lead you to anger and nowhere.

'Walk away' from people who deliberately put you down.

'Walk away' from any thought that reduces your worth.

'Walk away' from the failures and fears that stifle your dreams.

The more you 'walk away' from things that poison your soul, the happier your life will be.

Practice

'Walking' towards Happiness.

A New Lease of Life

A business executive was deep in debt and could see no way out. Creditors were closing in on him. Suppliers were demanding payment.

He sat on the park bench, head in hands, wondering if anything could save his company from bankruptcy.

Suddenly an old man appeared before him. "I can see that something is troubling you," he said. After listening to the executive's woes, the old man said, "I believe I can help you."

He asked the man his name, wrote out a cheque, and pushed it into his hand saying, "Take this money. Meet me here exactly one year from today, and you can pay me back at that time."

Then he turned and disappeared as quickly as he had come. The business executive saw in his hand a cheque for $500,000, signed by John D. Rockefeller, then one of the richest men in the world! "I can erase my money worries in an instant!" He realized. But instead, the executive decided to put the uncashed cheque in his safe. Just knowing it was there might give him the strength to work out a way to save his business, he thought.

With renewed optimism, he negotiated better deals and extended terms of payment. He closed several big sales. Within a few months, he was out of debt and making money once again.

Exactly one year later, he returned to the park with the uncashed cheque. At the agreed-upon time, the old man appeared.

But just as the executive was about to hand back the cheque and share his success story, a nurse came running up and grabbed the old man. "I'm so glad I caught him!" She cried. "I hope he hasn't been bothering you. He's always escaping from the mental asylum and telling people he's John D. Rockefeller." And she led the old man away by the arm.

The astonished executive just stood there, stunned. All year long he'd been wheeling and dealing, buying and selling, convinced he had half a million dollars behind him. Suddenly, he realized that it wasn't the money, real or imagined, that had turned his life around. It was his newfound self-confidence that gave him the power to achieve anything he ever imagined.

We know that GOD doesn't require us to "Be the Best"

He just wants us to "Do our Best"

And He will take care of the rest!

*　　　　*　　　　　　*　　　　　　**

Never think hard about past, it brings Tears...

Don't think much about future, it brings Fears...

Live this moment with a smile, it brings Cheers!!!

*　　　　*　　　　　　*　　　　　　**

Every test in our life makes us bitter or better,

Every problem comes to make us or break us,

Choice is ours whether we become victim or victorious!!!

The Second Chance

It was 25th January. Nisha was waiting for her husband Akshaye. It was their marriage anniversary. Things have got changed since their marriage. From the cute couple they turned into a fighting one. They quarreled everyday on every small thing. Nisha gave up thinking that Akshaye must have forgotten their anniversary and surely won't be back home on time. Akshaye too didn't like how the things were going. They were so loving, so caring before marriage. How everything got changed so radically.

It was 4:00 pm. The bell rang. Nisha was surprised. Akshaye finally remembered. She ran to open the door. Indeed Akshaye was standing outside. He was smiling and had a bunch of flowers in his hand. The two then started reliving their beautiful days, making up for their quarrels. There was champagne, light music and it was raining a little outside. Overall the weather too seemed to get romantic along with them.

But the moment came to a slight pause. The phone in the bedroom was ringing. Quite agitated, Nisha went to pick up the phone. It was a man on the other side. "Hello madam, I am calling from the police station. Is it Mr. Akshaye Malhotra's number?"

"Yeah, it is."

"There was an accident and a man died. We got your number from the man's purse. We need you to come here and identify the body."

Nisha's heart sank. "Whhhhaaat? B-but my husband is here with me."

"Sorry madam, the accident took place at 3:00 pm when the man was trying to board a bus."

Nisha was about to lose her senses. How could this happen? She knew this type of thing. She had heard about this. The soul of the person comes to meet you before it parts. She ran to the drawing room. Akshaye was not there. Is it true? Has something that bad really happened to Akshaye? Has he left her forever? Oh God, had she been given another chance, she would have mended all her faults. She rolled down on the floor awe struck.

Suddenly there was noise from the bathroom. Akshaye came out, "I forgot to tell you dear, my purse was stolen while I was returning home."

Life might not give you a second chance. So never waste a moment when you can make up for your deeds.

To be loved, be lovable.

*   *   *

Everyone wants happiness, no one wants pain,
But you can't have a rainbow, without a little rain.

*   *   *

Do not grieve that rose plants have thorns, rather rejoice that thorny bushes have roses.

Humanity

A nurse took the tired, anxious serviceman to the bedside. "Your son is here," she said to the old man. She had to repeat the words several times before the patient's eyes opened. Heavily sedated because of the pain of his heart attack, he dimly saw the young uniformed marine standing outside the oxygen tent. He reached out his hand. The marine wrapped his toughened fingers around the old man's limp ones, squeezing a message of love and encouragement.

The nurse brought a chair so that the marine could sit beside the bed. All through the night the young marine sat there in the poorly lit ward, holding the old man's hand and offering him words of love and strength. Occasionally, the nurse suggested that the marine move away and rest a while. He refused. Whenever the nurse came into the ward, the marine was oblivious of her and of the night noises of the hospital—the clanking of the oxygen tank, the laughter of the night staff members exchanging greetings, the cries and moans of the other patients. Now and then she heard him say a few gentle words. The dying man said nothing, only held tightly to his son all through the night.

Towards dawn, the old man died. The marine released the now lifeless hand he had been holding and went to tell the nurse. While she did what she had to do, he waited. Finally, she returned. She started to offer words of sympathy, but the marine interrupted her. "Who was that man?" He asked.

The nurse was startled, "He was your father," she answered.

"No, he wasn't," the marine replied. "I never saw him before in my life."

"Then why didn't you say something when I took you to him?"

"I knew right away there had been a mistake, but I also knew he needed his son, and his son just wasn't here. When I realized that he was too sick to tell whether or not I was his son, knowing how much he needed me, I stayed."

Living for self is part of Living;
Living for others is the Art of Living.

*   *   *

No Person in the World has
Ever been Rewarded
For what he has 'RECEIVED'...!
He is always "Honoured"
For what he has "GIVEN".

*   *   *

The loud voice of
Aarti in Temple
Namaz in Masjid
Prayer in Church
is heard by people, not by God.
GOD hears silent voice which comes from the heart!

I've Learned ...

I've learned ... That the best classroom in the world is at the feet of an elderly person.

I've learned ... That when you're in love, it shows.

I've learned ... That just one person saying to me, 'You've made my day!' makes my day.

I've learned ... That having a child fall asleep in your arms is one of the most peaceful feelings in the world.

I've learned ... That being kind is more important than being right.

I've learned ... That I can always pray for someone when I don't have the strength to help him in some other way.

I've learned ... That sometimes all a person needs is a hand to hold and a heart to understand.

I've learned ... That simple walks with my father around the block on summer nights when I was a child did wonders for me as an adult.

I've learned ... That money doesn't buy class.

I've learned ... That it's those small daily happenings that make life so spectacular.

I've learned ... That under everyone's hard shell is someone who wants to be appreciated and loved.

I've learned ... That to ignore the facts does not change the facts.

I've learned ... That when you plan to get even with someone, you are only letting that person continue to hurt you.

I've learned ... That love, not time, heals all wounds.

I've learned ... That the easiest way for me to grow as a person is to surround myself with people smarter than I am.

I've learned ... That no one is perfect until you fall in love with them.

I've learned ... That life is tough, but I'm tougher.

I've learned ... That opportunities are never lost; someone will take the ones you miss.

I've learned ... That when you harbor bitterness, happiness will dock elsewhere.

I've learned ... That a smile is an inexpensive way to improve your looks.

I've learned ... That when your newly born child/grandchild holds your little finger in his/her little fist, that you're hooked for life.

I've learned ... That everyone wants to live on top of the mountain, but all the happiness, and growth occurs while you're climbing it.

I've learned ... That the less time I have to work with, the more things I get done.

Mrs. Das divorced Mr. Das.

Now she's bin-das.

How much does a Teacher Make

The dinner guests were sitting around the table discussing life. One man, a CEO, decided to explain the problem with education. He argued, "What's a kid going to learn from someone who decided his best option in life was to become a teacher?"

To stress his point he said to another guest, "You're a teacher, Natasha. Be honest. What do you make?"

Natasha, who had a reputation for honesty and frankness replied, "You want to know what I make?"

She paused for a second, and then began...

"Well, I make kids work harder than they ever thought they could.

I make a C+ feel like the Olympic Gold Medal winner.

I make kids sit through 40 minutes of class time when their parents can't make them sit for 5 minutes without an I-Pod, Game Cube or Movie Rental.

You want to know what I make?"

She paused again and looked at each and every person at the table...

"I make kids wonder. I make them question.

I make them apologize and mean it. I make them have respect and take responsibility for their actions.

I teach them to write and then I make them write. Keyboarding isn't everything.

I make them read, read, read.

I make them show all their work in maths. They use their God given brain, not the man-made calculator.

I make my classroom a place where all my students feel safe.

Finally, I make them understand that if they use the gifts they were given, work hard, and follow their hearts, they can succeed in life."

Natasha paused one last time and then continued...

"Then, when people try to judge me by what I make, with me knowing money isn't everything, I can hold my head up high and pay no attention because they are ignorant.

You want to know what I make.

I MAKE A DIFFERENCE.

What do you make Mr. CEO?"

A young newly appointed company's manager made a deal, in which his company lost one million rupees.

He came to the office, feeling his guilt and not waiting until the owner would tell him something, said: "I understand that you can sack me, and I, admitting my guilt, accept your decision."

"To sack you?" The leader said: "I have just spent one million on your training and may not throw such valuable human resource. Go to work!"

The Mirror's Fault

I look in the mirror
And what do I see?
A strange looking person
That cannot be me.

For I am much younger
And not nearly so fat
As that face in the mirror
I am looking at.

Oh, where are the mirrors
That I used to know
Like the ones which were
Made thirty years ago?

Now all things have changed
And I'm sure you'll agree
Mirrors are not as good
As they used to be.

So never be concerned
If wrinkles appear
For one thing I've learned
Which is very clear.

Should your complexion
Be less than perfection
It is really the mirror
That needs correction!!!

Lunch with God

A little boy wanted to meet God. He knew it was a long trip to where God lived, so he packed his suitcase with potato chips and orange juice and started his journey.

When he had gone about three blocks, he met an old woman. She was sitting in the park, just staring at some pigeons. The boy sat down next to her and opened his suitcase. He was about to take juice when he noticed that the old lady looked hungry, so he offered her some chips. She gratefully accepted it and smiled at him.

Her smile was so pretty that the boy wanted to see it again, so he offered her juice. Again, she smiled at him. The boy was delighted. They sat there all afternoon eating and smiling, but they never said a word.

As twilight approached, the boy realized how tired he was and he got up to leave; but before he had gone more than a few steps, he turned around, ran back to the old woman, and gave her a hug. She gave him her biggest smile ever. When the boy opened the door of his house a short time later, his mother was surprised by the look of joy on his face. She asked him, "What did you do today that made you so happy?" He replied, "I had lunch with God." But before his mother could respond, he added, "You know what? She's got the most beautiful smile I've ever seen!"

Meanwhile, the old woman, also radiant with joy, returned to her home. Her son was stunned by the look of peace on her face and he asked, "Mother, what did you do today that made you so happy?" She replied, "I ate potato chips in the park with God." However, before her son responded, she added, "You know, he's much younger than I expected."

Who can Understand Love

Once upon a time, there was an island where all the feelings lived—Happiness, Sadness, Knowledge, and all others, including Love. One day it was announced to the feelings that the island would sink, so all constructed boats and left.

Love was the only one who stayed. Love wanted to hold out until the last possible moment. When the island had almost sunk, Love decided to ask for help. Richness was passing by Love in a grand boat. Love said, "Richness, can you take me with you?" Richness answered, "No, I can't. There is a lot of gold and silver in my boat. There is no place here for you."

Love decided to ask Vanity who was also passing by in a beautiful vessel. "Vanity, please help me!" "I can't help you. You are all wet and might damage my boat," Vanity replied.

Sadness was close by so Love asked, "Sadness, let me go with you." "Oh ... Love, I am so sad that I need to be by myself!" Happiness passed by Love, too, but she was so happy that she did not even hear when Love called her.

Suddenly, there was a voice, "Come, Love, I will take you." It was an elder. When they arrived at dry land, the elder went his own way. Love asked Knowledge, another elder, "Who Helped me?"

"It was Time," Knowledge answered.

"Time?" Asked Love. "But why did Time help me?" Knowledge smiled with deep wisdom and answered, "Because only Time is capable of understanding how valuable Love is."

Happy Improvement

A super-deluxe hotel group had invited Mr. Masai from Japan to hold a workshop for its staff. The staff were very skeptical—the hotel is doing excellent business, this person from Japan has no exposure to hotel industry—what exactly is he going to teach?

But everybody as planned gathered for the workshop in the conference hall sharp at 9 am. Mr. Masai was introduced to them—a not so impressive personality, nor the English all that good; spoke as if he was first formulating each sentence in Japanese and then translating it into rather clumsy English.

"Good morning! Let's start work. I am told this is a workshop; but I see neither work nor shop. So let's proceed where work is happening. Let's start with the first room on the first floor." Mr. Masai, followed by the senior management and the participants, proceeded to the destination. That happened to be the laundry room of the hotel. Mr. Masai entered the room and stood at the window. "Beautiful view!" He said. The staff knew it; they need not invite a Japanese consultant to tell them this!

"A room with such a beautiful view is being wasted as a laundry room. Shift the laundry to the basement and convert this into a guest room." Aa haa! Now nobody had ever thought about that!

The manager said, "Yes, it can be done."

"Then let's do it." Mr. Masai said.

"Yes sir, I will make a note of this and we will include it in the report on the workshop," replied the manager.

"Excuse me, but there is nothing to note down in this. Let's just do it, just now," said Mr. Masai.

"Just now?" Asked the Manager.

"Yes, decide on a room on the ground floor/basement and shift the stuff out of this room right away. It should take a couple of hours, right?" Said Mr. Masai.

"Yes." Replied the Manager.

"Let's come back here just before lunch. By then all this stuff will have got shifted out and the room must be ready with the carpets, furniture, etc. and from today you can start earning the few thousand that you charge your customers for a room per night."

"Ok, Sir." The manager had no option.

The next destination was the pantry. At the entrance were two huge sinks full of plates to be washed. Mr. Masai removed his jacket and started washing the plates.

"Sir, please, what are you doing?" The manager didn't know what to say and what to do.

"Why, I am washing the plates", replied Mr. Masai.

"But sir, there is staff here to do that." Said the Manager.

Mr. Masai continued washing, "I think sink is for washing plates, there are stands here to keep the plates and the plates should go into the stands."

All the officials wondered—did they require a consultant to tell them this?

After finishing the job, Mr. Masai asked, "how many plates do you have?"

"Plenty, so that there should never be any shortage." Replied the Manager.

Mr. Masai said, "We have a word in Japanese—'Muda'. Muda means delay, muda means unnecessary spending. One lesson to be learned in this workshop is to avoid both. If you have plenty of plates, there will be delay in cleaning them up. The first step to correct this situation is to remove all the excess plates."

"Yes, we will say this in the report." Said the Manager.

"No, wasting our time in writing the report is again an instance of 'muda'. We must pack the extra plates in a box right away and send these to whichever other section of the hotel requires these. Throughout the workshop now we will find out where all we find this 'muda' hidden."

And then at every spot and session, the staff eagerly awaited to find out muda and learn how to avoid it.

On the last day, Mr. Masai told a story. "A Japanese and an American, both fond of hunting, entered a jungle with guns. In the pursuit of game they entered deep jungle and suddenly realized that they had run out of bullets. Just then they heard a lion roaring. Both started running. But the Japanese took a short break to put on his sports shoes. The American said, "What are you doing? We must first get to the car." The Japanese said, "No. I only have to ensure that I remain ahead of you." All the participants engrossed in listening to the story, realized suddenly that the lion would stop after getting his victim!

"The lesson is, competition in today's world is so fierce, that it is important to stay ahead of others, even by just a couple of steps. And you have such a huge and naturally well endowed country. If you remember to curtail your production expenditure and give the best quality always, you will be miles ahead as compared to so many other countries in the world.", concluded Mr. Masai.

Don't Hope, Decide!

While waiting to pick up a friend at the airport, I had one of those life-changing experiences that you hear other people talk about—the kind that sneaks up on you unexpectedly. This one occurred a mere two feet away from me.

Straining to locate my friend among the passengers, I noticed a man coming toward me carrying two light bags. He stopped right next to me to greet his family.

First he motioned to his son (maybe six years old) as he laid down his bags. They gave each other a long, loving hug. As they separated enough to look in each other's face, I heard the father say, "It's so good to see you, son. I missed you so much!" His son smiled somewhat shyly, averted his eyes and replied softly, "Me too, Dad!"

While this was happening, a baby girl (perhaps one or one-and-a-half) was squirming excitedly in her mother's arms, never once taking her little eyes off the wonderful sight of her returning father. The man said, "Hi, baby girl!" As he gently took the child from her mother. He quickly kissed her face all over and then held her close to his chest while rocking her from side to side. The little girl instantly relaxed and simply laid her head on his shoulder, motionless in pure contentment.

After several moments, he handed his daughter to his son and gazed into his wife's eyes for several seconds and then silently mouthed. "I love you so much!" They stared at each other's eyes, beaming big smiles at one another, while holding both hands.

For an instant they reminded me of newlyweds, but I knew by the presence of their kids that they couldn't possibly be. I puzzled about it for a moment then realized how totally engrossed I was in the wonderful display of unconditional love not more than an arm's length away from me. I suddenly felt uncomfortable, as if I was invading something sacred, but was amazed to hear my own voice nervously ask, "Wow! How long have you two been married?"

"Been together twelve years total." He replied, without breaking his gaze from his lovely wife's face.

"Well then, how long have you been away?" I asked.

The man finally turned and looked at me, still beaming his joyous smile. "Two whole days!"

Two days? I was stunned. By the intensity of the greeting, I had assumed he'd been gone for at least several weeks, if not months. I know my expression betrayed me.

I said almost offhandedly, hoping to end my intrusion with some semblance of grace, "I hope my marriage is still that passionate after twelve years!"

The man suddenly stopped smiling. He looked me straight in the eye, and with forcefulness that burned right into my soul, he told me something that left me a different person. He told me, "Don't hope, friend… decide!" Then he flashed me his wonderful smile again, shook my hand and said, "God bless!"

An artist made a beautiful painting of heart. Then he drew a small door in it. But there was no handle in the door. Somebody asked the artist, why he had not made the handle. The artist replied, "the doors of the heart open from inside, not from outside".

Do You Build Bridges or Fences

Once upon a time, two brothers, who lived on adjoining farms, fell into conflict. It was the first serious rift in 40 years of farming side by side, sharing machinery, and trading labor and goods as needed without a conflict.

Then the long collaboration fell apart. It began with a small misunderstanding and it grew into a major difference, and finally it exploded into an exchange of bitter words followed by weeks of silence.

One morning there was a knock on the elder brother's door. He opened it to find a man with a carpenter's tool box.

"I'm looking for a few days' work." He said. "Perhaps you would have a few small jobs here and there I could help with?"

"Yes." Said the elder brother. "I do have a job for you. Look across the creek at that farm. That's my neighbor; in fact, it's my younger brother. Last week there was a meadow between us and he joined it to the nearby river and now there is a waterbody between us. Well, he may have done this to spite me, but I'll do him one better. I want you to build me a fence, an 8-foot fence, so I won't need to see his place or his face anymore."

The carpenter said, "I think I understand the situation. Give me the material and I'll be able to do a job that pleases you."

The older brother had to go to town, so he helped the carpenter get the material ready and then he was off for the day.

The carpenter worked hard all that day measuring, sawing, nailing. About sunset when the farmer returned, the carpenter had just finished his job.

The farmer's eyes opened wide, his jaw dropped. There was no fence there at all. It was a bridge—a bridge stretching from one side of the creek to the other! A fine piece of work, handrails and all—and the neighbor, his younger brother, was coming toward them, his arms outstretched. "You are quite a fellow to build this bridge after all I've said and done."

The two brothers stood at each end of the bridge, and then they met in the middle, taking each other's hand.

They turned to see the carpenter hoist his toolbox onto his shoulder.

"No, wait! Stay a few days. I've a lot of other projects for you," said the older brother.

"I'd love to stay on," the carpenter said, "but I have many more bridges to build."

A lot of trouble would disappear
If only people would learn to talk to one another
Instead of talking about one another.

*   *   *

Give thousand chances to your enemy to become your friend.
But don't give a single chance to your friend to become your enemy.

*   *   *

Smile when picking up the phone. The caller will hear it in your voice.

Love Her ...

Love her ... when she sips on your coffee or tea. She only wants to make sure it tastes just right for you.

Love her ... when she "pushes" you to pray. She wants to be with you in Jannat (Paradise).

Love her ... when she is jealous. Out of all the men she can have, she chose you.

Love her ... when she has annoying little habits that drives you nuts. You have them too.

Love her ... when her cooking is bad. She tries.

Love her ... when she looks dishevelled in the morning. She always grooms herself up again.

Love her ... when she asks to help with the kids homework. She only wants you to be part of the home.

Love her ... when she asks if she looks fat. Your opinion counts, so tell her she's beautiful.

Love her ... when she looks beautiful. She's yours so appreciate her.

Love her ... when she spends hours to get ready. She only wants to look her best for you.

Love her ... when she cries for absolutely nothing. Don't ask, tell her it is going to be okay.

Love her ... when she tells you how to drive. She only wants you to be safe.

Love her ... when she argues. She only wants to make things right for both.

Love her ... she is yours. You don't need any other special reason!!!

Things God won't Ask on that Day

God won't ask what kind of car you drove. He'll ask how many people you drove who didn't have transportation.

God won't ask the square footage of your house. He'll ask how many people you welcomed into your home.

God won't ask about the clothes you had in your closet. He'll ask how many you helped to clothe.

God won't ask what your highest salary was. He'll ask if you compromised your character to obtain it.

God won't ask what your job title was. He'll ask if you performed your job to the best of your ability.

God won't ask how many friends you had. He'll ask how many people to whom you were a friend.

God won't ask in what neighborhood you lived. He'll ask how you treated your neighbors.

God won't ask about the color of your skin. He'll ask about the content of your character.

God won't ask why it took you so long to seek salvation. He'll lovingly take you to your mansion in heaven, and not to the gates of hell.

The purpose of life is, a life of purpose.

*   *   *

Kindness: *A language the deaf can hear, the blind can see and the mute can speak.*

Date with a Woman …

After 21 years of marriage, my wife wanted me to take another woman out for dinner and a movie. She said, "I love you but I know this other woman loves you and would love to spend some time with you."

The other woman that my wife wanted me to visit was my mother, who has been a widow for 19 years, but the demands of my work and my three children had made it possible to visit her only occasionally.

That night I called to invite her to go out for dinner and a movie.

"What's wrong, are you well?" She asked.

My mother is the type of woman who suspects that a late night call or a surprise invitation is a sign of bad news.

"I thought that it would be pleasant to be with you," I responded, "Just the two of us."

She thought about it for a moment, and then said, "I would like that very much."

That Friday after work, as I drove over to pick her up, I was a bit nervous. When I arrived at her house, I noticed that she too seemed to be nervous about our date. She waited at the door with her coat on. She had curled her hair and was wearing the dress that she had worn to celebrate her last wedding anniversary.

She smiled from a face that was as radiant as an angel's. "I told my friends that I was going to go out with my son, and they were impressed," She said, as she got into the car. "They can't wait to hear about our meeting."

We went to a restaurant that was nice and cozy. My mother took my arm as if she were the First Lady.

During the dinner, we had an agreeable conversation, nothing extraordinary, but catching up on recent events of each other's life. We talked so much that we missed the movie. As we arrived at her house later, she said, "I'll go out with you again, but only if you let me invite you." I agreed.

"How was your dinner date?" Asked my wife when I reached home.

"Very nice. Much more so than I could have imagined," I answered.

A few days later, my mother died of a massive heart attack. It happened so suddenly that I didn't have time to do anything for her. Sometime later, I received an envelope with a copy of a restaurant receipt from the same place mother and I had dined. An attached note said: "I paid this bill in advance. I wasn't sure that I could be there; but nevertheless, I paid for two plates; one for you and the other for your wife. You will never know what that night meant for me. I love you, my son."

The most wonderful places to be in the world are:

In someone's thoughts.

In someone's prayers.

In someone's heart.

Moment

In a forest, a pregnant deer is about to give birth to a baby. It finds a remote grass field nearby a river and slowly goes there thinking it would be safe. As she moves slowly, she gets labour pain.

At the same moment, dark clouds gather around that area and lightning starts a forest fire. Turning left, she sees a hunter who is aiming an arrow from a distance. As she tries to move towards right, she spots a hungry lion approaching towards her.

What can the pregnant deer do, as she is already under labour pain?

What do you think will happen?

Will the deer survive?

Will it give birth to a fawn?

Will the fawn survive?

OR

Will everything be burnt by the forest fire?

Can the deer go left? No, the hunter's arrow is pointing at her.

Can she go right? No, the hungry male lion is approaching her.

Can she move up? No, there the forest is on fire.

Can she move down? No, that is where the fierce river is.

Answer: She does nothing. She just focuses on giving birth to a new LIFE.

The sequence of events that happen at that fraction of a second (moment) are as follows:

In a spur of a *moment*, a lightning strikes, and blinds the eyes of the hunter!

At that *moment*, he releases the arrow missing and zipping past the deer, hitting and injuring the lion badly!

At that *moment*, it starts to rain heavily and puts out the forest fire!

At that *moment*, the deer gives birth to a healthy fawn!

In our life too, there are *moments* of *choice* when we all have to deal with negative thoughts from all sides. Some thoughts are so powerful they overcome us, and make us clueless.

Anything can happen in a *moment* in this life. If you are religious, superstitious, atheist, agnostic or whatever, you can attribute this *moment* to divine intervention, faith, sudden luck, serendipity, coincidence, *karma*, or a simply 'I just don't know!'

The priority of the deer, in that given moment, was simply giving birth to a baby, because life is precious!

"LIFE is flowing like a river,
With unexpected TURNS,
May be GOOD,
May be BAD.
Learn to enjoy each Turn
because these Turns
Never RE-TURN."

Don't Take Them for Granted

We take everything for granted
- A constantly worried mom
- A strict dad
- An annoying brother
- A rude sister
- A *chipku* friend
- A demanding wife
- A complaining husband...

BUT

when we lose them, then we miss them as:
- My caring mom
- My concerned dad
- My best brother
- My loving sister
- My real friend
- My wife, my life
- My hubby, my world.

Don't take them for granted!

If your eyes are positive, you will like the world.

If your tongue is positive, the world will like you.

Man with Four Wives

There was a man with four wives. He loved his fourth wife the most and took great care of her and gave her the best.

He also loved his third wife and always wanted to show her off to his friends. However, he always had a fear that she might run away with some other man.

He loved his second wife too. Whenever he faced some problems, he always turned to his second wife and she would always help him out.

He did not love his first wife though she loved him deeply, was very loyal to him and took great care of him.

One day the man fell very ill and knew that he is going to die soon. He told himself, "I have four wives with me. I will take one of them along with me when I die to keep company in my death."

Thus, he asked the fourth wife to die along with him and give company. "No way!" She replied and walked away without another word.

He asked his third wife. She said "Life is so good over here. I'm going to remarry when you die."

He then asked his second wife. She said "I'm Sorry. I can't help you this time around. At the most I can only accompany you till your grave."

By now his heart sank and turned cold. Then a voice called out: "I'll leave with you. I'll follow you no matter where you go." The man looked up and there was his first wife. She was so skinny, almost like she suffered from malnutrition. Greatly grieved, the man said, "I should have taken much better care of you while I could have!"

Actually, we all have four wives in our lives.

a. The fourth wife is our body. No matter how much time and effort we lavish in making it look good, it'll leave us when we die.

b. The third wife is our possessions, status and wealth. When we die, they go to others.

c. The second wife is our family and friends. No matter how close they had been there for us when we're alive, the furthest they can stay by us is up to the grave.

d. The first wife is the our soul, neglected in our pursuit of material wealth and pleasure.

What's the Secret of Success?

I found the answer in my room.

The fan said: Be cool.

The roof said: Aim high.

The window said: Open up to the world.

The door said: Push the troubles.

The clock said: Every minute is precious.

The mirror said: Reflect before you act.

The lamp said: Make light for your future.

The calendar said: Be up-to-date.

Friend

A bond of love,

A medal of trust.

A shoulder in sadness,

A hand in darkness.

A special relation to hold,

An ear where secrets can be told.

An appreciator for encouragement,

Something that doesn't cost.

A jewel never to be lost.

Is the magic called

F R I E N D !

One good book is equal to hundred friends but one good friend is equal to a library.

               *   *   *

True friends have a character like salt, their presence may not be remembered but their absence makes all things tasteless.

My Favourite Philosophy

A man with one watch knows what time it is, a man with two watches is never quite sure.

Look at life through the windshield, not the rearview mirror.

People may doubt what you say, but they will believe what you do.

Be nice to people on your way up, because you'll need them on your way down.

Never explain. Your friends do not need it and your enemies will not believe it.

While seeking revenge, dig two graves—one for yourself.

Time you enjoyed wasting was not wasted.

Courage is not a lack of fear, but the ability to act while facing fear.

You've got to do your own growing, no matter how tall your father was.

The best way to predict your future is to create it!

A wise old owl sat on oak,

The more he saw the less he spoke.

The less he spoke the more he heard,

Why are we not like that wise old bird?

Worth it!

Horror gripped the heart of the soldier as he saw his lifelong friend fall in battle. Caught in a trench with continuous gunfire whizzing over his head, the soldier asked his lieutenant if he might go out into the "no man's land" between the trenches to bring his fallen comrade back.

"You can go," said the lieutenant, "but I don't think it will be worth it. Your friend is probably dead and you may throw your life away." The lieutenant's advice didn't matter, and the soldier went anyway. Miraculously he managed to reach his friend, hoist him onto his shoulder and bring him back to their company's trench. As the two of them tumbled in together to the bottom of the trench, the officer checked the wounded soldier, and then looked kindly at his friend.

"I told you it wouldn't be worth it," he said. "Your friend is dead and you are mortally wounded."

"It was worth it, though, sir," said the soldier.

"What do you mean worth it?" Responded the Lieutenant. "Your friend is dead."

"Yes Sir" the private answered. "But it was worth it because when I got to him, he was still alive and I had the satisfaction of hearing him saying, "Sanjay, I knew you'd come."

> *Once all villagers decided to pray for rain. On the day of prayer all the people gathered but only one girl came with an umbrella.*
>
> *That's Faith!*

True Love

The passengers on the bus watched sympathetically as the attractive young woman with the white cane made her way carefully up the steps. She paid the conductor, and using her hands to feel the location of the seats, walked down the aisle and found the seat he'd told her was empty. Then she settled in, placed her briefcase on her lap and rested her cane against her leg.

It had been a year since Priya, 34, became blind due to a medical misdiagnosis. She had been rendered sightless, and she was suddenly thrown into a world of darkness, anger, frustration and self-pity. And all she had to cling to was her husband, Anil.

Anil was an Air Force officer and he loved Priya with all his heart. When she first lost her sight, he watched her sink into despair and was determined to help his wife gain the strength and confidence she needed to become independent again.

Finally, Priya felt ready to return to her job, but how would she get there? She used to take the bus, but was now too frightened to get around the city by herself. Anil volunteered to drive her to work each day, even though they worked at opposite ends of the city. At first, this comforted Priya, and fulfilled Anil's need to protect his sightless wife who was so insecure about performing the slightest task. Soon, however, Anil realized the arrangement wasn't working. Priya is going to have to start taking the bus again, he admitted to himself. But she was still so fragile, how would she react?

Just as he predicted, Priya was horrified at the idea of taking the bus again. "I'm blind!," she responded bitterly. "How am I supposed to know where I am going? I feel like you're abandoning me."

Anil's heart broke to hear these words, but he knew what had to be done. He promised Priya that each morning and evening he would ride the bus with her, for as long as it took, until she got the hang of it. And that is exactly what happened. For two solid weeks, Anil, military uniform and all, accompanied Priya to and from work each day. He taught her how to rely on her other senses, specifically her hearing, to determine where she was and how to adapt to her new environment. He helped her befriend the bus drivers who could watch out for her, and save her a seat.

Finally, Priya decided that she was ready to try the trip on her own. Monday morning arrived, and before she left, she threw her arms around Anil, her temporary bus-riding companion, her husband, and her best friend. Her eyes filled with tears of gratitude for his loyalty, his patience, and his love. She said good-bye, and for the first time, they went their separate ways. Monday, Tuesday, Wednesday, Thursday… each day on her own went perfectly, and Priya had never felt better. She was doing it! She was going to work all by herself.

On Friday morning, Priya took the bus to work as usual. As she was paying the fare to exit the bus, the driver said, "Boy, I sure do envy you." Priya wasn't sure if the driver was speaking to her or not. After all, who on earth would ever envy a blind woman who had struggled just to find the courage to live for the past year?

Curious, she asked the driver, "Why do you say that you envy me?" The driver responded, "It must feel good to be taken care of and protected like you are."

Priya had no idea what the driver was talking about, and again asked, "What do you mean?"

The driver answered, "You know, every morning for the past week, a fine-looking gentleman in a military uniform has been standing across the corner watching you as you get off the bus. He makes sure you cross the street safely and he watches until you enter your office building. Then he blows you a kiss, gives you a little salute and walks away. You are one lucky lady."

Tears of happiness poured down Priya's cheeks. For although she couldn't physically see him, she had always felt Anil's presence. She was lucky, so lucky, for he had given her a gift more powerful than sight, a gift she didn't need to see to believe, the gift of love that can bring light where there is darkness.

If you want Happiness

For an hour	—	*Eat good food*
For a day	—	*Go for a picnic*
For a month	—	*Go for a long vacation*
For a year	—	*Inherit a fortune*
For many years	—	*Love someone*
For a lifetime	—	*Help someone.*

Value what is Yours

The owner of a small business, a friend of a great poet, met him on the street and asked him, "I need to sell my small farm, the one you know so well. Could you please write an advertisement for me for the paper?"

The poet wrote:

"For sale, a beautiful property, where birds sing at dawn in extensive woodland, bisected by the brilliant and sparkling waters of a large stream. The house is bathed by the rising sun. It offers tranquil shade in the evenings in the veranda."

Some time later, the poet met his friend and asked whether he had sold the property.

To which the friend replied: "I've changed my mind. When I read what you had written, I realized the treasure that was mine!"

While you're hating your life just because you can't get what you want,

Remember that someone is praying to have a life like yours.

Let it be

Once Buddha was travelling with a few of his followers. While they were passing a lake, Buddha told one of his disciples, "I am thirsty. Do get me some water from the lake."

The disciple walked up to the lake. At that moment, a bullock cart started crossing through the lake. As a result, the water became very muddy. The disciple thought, "How can I give this muddy water to Buddha to drink?"

So he came back and told Buddha, "The water in there is very muddy. I don't think it is fit to drink."

After some time, again Buddha asked the same disciple to go back to the lake. The disciple went back, and found that the water was still muddy. He returned and informed Buddha about the same.

After around fifteen minutes, again Buddha asked the same disciple to go back. This time, the disciple found the mud had settled down, and the water was clean and clear. So he collected some water in a pot and brought it to Buddha.

Buddha looked at the water, and then he looked up at the disciple and said, "See what you did to make the water clean. You let it be, and the mud settled down on its own—and you have clear water.

Your mind is like that too! When it is disturbed, just let it be. Give it a little time. It will settle down on its own. You don't have to put in any effort to calm it down. It will happen. It is effortless."

Moral: Having 'Peace of Mind' is not a strenuous job; it is an effortless process!

God's Wings

After a forest fire in a National Park, forest rangers began their trek up a mountain to assess the inferno's damage. One ranger found a bird literally petrified in ashes, perched statuesquely on the ground at the base of a tree. Somewhat sickened by the eerie sight, he knocked over the bird with a stick. When he gently struck it, three tiny chicks scurried from under their dead mother's wings.

The loving mother, keenly aware of impending disaster, had carried her offsprings to the base of the tree and had gathered them under her wings, instinctively knowing that the toxic smoke would rise. She could have flown to safety but had refused to abandon her babies. Then the blaze had arrived and the heat had scorched her small body. The mother had remained steadfast, because she had been willing to die, so those under the cover of her wings would live.

> *Do all the good you can*
>
> *By all the means you can*
>
> *In all the ways you can*
>
> *In all the places you can*
>
> *At all the times you can*
>
> *To all the people you can*
>
> *As long as ever you can.*

Not as Happy as You

Sometimes in life
We feel so blue,
But someone, somewhere
is not as happy as you.

Somewhere far at the border
When a soldier sleeps,
Missing his loved ones
He silently weeps.

Somewhere a mother
Painfully sighs,
Because her new born baby
Didn't open her eyes.

Somewhere a poor dad
Silently cries,
When he sees his son
Begging for a bowl of rice.

Somewhere in an orphanage
A little girl is sad,
When she misses her
Mom and dad.

So at times
A reason to smile you may not have any,
Say to yourself that
You're happier than many.

Anger is Danger

There once was a little boy who had a bad temper. His father gave him a bag of nails and told him that every time he lost his temper, he must hammer a nail into the fence.

The first day the boy had driven 37 nails into the fence. Over the next few weeks as he learned to control his anger, the number of nails hammered daily, gradually dwindled down. He discovered it was easier to hold his temper than to drive those nails into the fence. Finally the day came when the boy didn't lose his temper at all. He told his father about it and the father suggested that the boy now pull out one nail for each day that he was able to hold his temper.

The days passed and the young boy was finally able to tell his father that all the nails were gone. The father took his son by the hand and led him to the fence. He said "You have done well, my son, but look at the holes in the fence. The fence will never be the same. When you say things in anger, they leave a scar just like this one."

Relations are like stapler pins. Easy to attach, hard to detach. And when pin is removed, it always leaves a mark. So take care!

*   *   *

No matter how many times the Teeth bite the Tongue, They still stay together in one Mouth;

That is the Spirit of 'Forgiveness'!!!

Salted Coffee

He met her at a party. She was so outstanding, many guys looking at her admiringly, while he was so normal, nobody paid attention to him. At the end of the party, he invited her to have coffee with him. She was surprised but due to being polite, she agreed. They sat in a nice coffee shop. He was too nervous to say anything, she felt uncomfortable, and thought to herself, "Please, let me go home..."

Suddenly he asked the waiter, "Would you please give me some salt? I'd like to put it in my coffee." Everybody stared at him, so strange! His face turned red but still, he put the salt in his coffee and drank it.

She asked him curiously, "Why do you have this strange taste?"

He replied, "When I was a little boy, I lived near the sea, I liked playing in the sea, I could feel the taste of the sea, just like the taste of the salty coffee. Now every time I have the salty coffee, I always think of my childhood, think of my hometown. I miss my hometown so much. I miss my parents who are still living there."

While saying that tears filled his eyes. She was deeply touched. That's his true feeling, from the bottom of his heart. A man who can tell out his homesickness, he must be a man who loves home, cares about home, has responsibility of home. Then she also started to speak, spoke about her faraway hometown, her childhood, her family.

That was a really nice talk, also a beautiful beginning of their story. They continued to date. She found that actually he was a man who meets all her demands; he had tolerance, was kind hearted, warm, cheerful. He was such a good person but she almost missed him! Thanks to his salty coffee!

Then the story was just like every beautiful love story, the princess married the prince, and then they were living the happy life... and, every time she made coffee for him, she put some salt in the coffee, as she knew that's the way he liked it.

After 40 years, he passed away, left her a letter which said, "My dearest, please forgive me, forgive my whole life's lie. This was the only lie I said to you—the salty coffee. Remember the first time we dated? I was so nervous at that time, actually I wanted some sugar, but I said salt. It was hard for me to change so I just went ahead. I never thought that could be the start of our communication!

I tried to tell you the truth many times in my life, but I was too afraid to do that, as I have promised not to lie to you for anything. Now I'm dying, I am afraid of nothing so I tell you the truth, I don't like the salty coffee, what a strange bad taste. But I have had the salty coffee for my whole life! Since I knew you, I never feel sorry for anything I do for you. Having you with me is my biggest happiness for my whole life. If I can live for the second time, still want to know you and have you for my whole life, even though I have to drink the salty coffee again."

Her tears made the letter totally wet. Someday, someone asked her, "What's the taste of salty coffee?"

She replied, "It's sweet."

Never let your friends feel lonely.
Disturb them at all times.

Be a Lake

The old Master instructed an unhappy young man to put a handful of salt in a glass of water and then to drink it.

"How does it taste?" The Master asked.

"Awful," spat the apprentice.

The Master chuckled and then asked the young man to take another handful of salt and put it in a lake. The two walked in silence to the nearby lake and when the apprentice swirled his handful of salt into the lake, the old man said, "Now drink from the lake."

As the water dripped down the young man's chin, the Master asked, "How does it taste?"

"Good!" Remarked the apprentice.

"Do you taste the salt?" Asked the Master.

"No," said the young man.

The Master sat beside this troubled young man, took his hands, and said, "The pain of life is pure salt; no more, no less. The amount of pain in life remains the same, exactly the same. But the amount we taste the 'pain' depends on the container we put it into.

So when you are in pain, the only thing you can do is to enlarge your sense of things ...

Stop being a Glass, become a LAKE!

Let's Change Our Vision

There was a millionaire who was infected by severe eye pain. He consulted many physicians and took lots of medicines and injections. But the ache persisted. At last a monk who was supposed to be an expert in treating such patients was called for. The monk understood his problem and said that for sometime he should concentrate only on green colour and not fall his eyes on any other colour.

The millionaire got together a group of painters and purchased barrels of green color and directed that every object his eye was likely to fall to be painted in green colour.

When the monk came to visit him after few days, the millionaire's servants ran with buckets of green paint and poured on him since he was wearing a red dress, lest their master not see any colour other than green.

The monk laughed and said "If only you had purchased a pair of green spectacles, worth just a few rupees, you could have saved these walls and pots and all other articles and also could have saved a large share of your fortune. You cannot paint the world green."

Let us change how we see and the world will appear accordingly. It is foolish to shape the world, let us shape ourselves first.

Let's change our vision!

As cold water and warm iron take away the wrinkles of clothes, a cool mind and warm heart takes out the worries of life.

Why do We Shout when We are Angry

A Hindu saint who was visiting river Ganges to take bath found a group of family members on the bank, shouting in anger at each other. He turned to his disciples and asked, "Why do people shout at each other when they are angry?"

Disciples thought for a while, one of them said, "Because we lose our calm, we shout."

"But why should you shout when the other person is standing just next to you? You can as well tell him what you have to say in a soft manner." Said the saint.

Disciples gave some answers but none satisfied the saint. Finally he explained, "When two people are angry at each other, their hearts distance a lot. To cover that distance they must shout to be able to hear each other. The angrier they are, the stronger they will have to shout to hear each other to cover that great distance."

"What happens when two people fall in love? They don't shout at each other but talk softly, because their hearts are very close. The distance between them is either nonexistent or very small…" the saint continued, "When they love each other even more, what happens? They do not speak, only whisper and they get even closer to each other in their love. Finally they even need not whisper, they only look at each other and that's all. That is how close two people are when they love each other."

He looked at his disciples and said. "So when you argue do not let your hearts gain distance, do not say words that widen the gap, or else there will come a day when the distance is so great that you will not find the path to return."

Address of God

Once upon a time, when God had finished making the world, he wanted to leave behind a piece of His own divinity, a spark of His essence, a promise to man of what he could become, with effort. He looked for a place to hide this precious gift because, He explained, what man could find too easily would never be valued by him.

"Then you must hide this gift on the highest mountain peak on earth," said one of His counselors.

God shook His head, "No, for man is an adventuresome creature and he will soon learn to climb the highest mountain peaks."

"Hide it then, My Lord, in the depths of the earth."

"I think not," said God, "for man will one day discover that he can dig into the deepest parts of the earth."

"In the middle of the ocean then, God?"

God shook His head. "I've given man a brain, you see, and one day he'll learn to build ships and cross the mightiest oceans."

"Where then, My Lord?" Cried His counselors.

God smiled, "I'll hide it where every man and woman will be able to find it if they look sincerely and deeply enough. I'll hide it in their heart, because that's the place where LOVE resides..."

> *Prayer is not a "spare wheel" that you pull out when in trouble, but it is a "steering wheel" that directs the right path throughout.*

Hindering Growth

One day, when all the employees reached their office, they saw a notice on the door on which it was written:

Yesterday the person who has been hindering your growth in this company passed away. We invite you to join the funeral in the conference room.

In the beginning, they all got sad for the death of one of their colleagues, but after a while they started getting curious to know who was that man who hindered the growth of his colleagues and the company itself.

Everyone thought: Who is this guy who was hindering my progress? Well, at last he died!

One by one the employees got closer to the coffin, and when they looked inside it they suddenly became speechless. They stood nearby the coffin, shocked and in silence, as if someone had touched the deepest part of their soul.

There was a mirror inside the coffin, everyone who looked inside it could see himself. There was also a sign next to the mirror that said:

There is only one person who is capable to set limits to your growth: IT IS YOU. Your life does not change when your boss changes, when your friends change, when your company changes. Your life changes when YOU CHANGE, when you go beyond your limiting beliefs, when you realize that you are the only one responsible for your life. You are the only person who can influence your happiness and your success. You are the only person who can help yourself!

The Three Trees

Once there were three trees on a hill in the woods. They were discussing their hopes and dreams when the first tree said, "Someday I hope to be a treasure chest. I could be filled with gold, silver and precious gems. I could be decorated with intricate carving and everyone would see the beauty."

Then the second tree said, "Someday I will be a mighty ship. I will take kings and queens across the waters and sail to the corners of the world. Everyone will feel safe in me because of the strength of my hull."

Finally the third tree said, "I want to grow to be the tallest and straightest tree in the forest. People will see me on top of the hill and look up to my branches, and think of the heavens and God and how close to them I am reaching. I will be the greatest tree of all time and people will always remember me."

After a few years of praying that their dreams would come true, a group of woodsmen came upon the trees.

When one came to the first tree he said, "This looks like a strong tree, I think I should be able to sell the wood to a carpenter," and he began cutting it down. The tree was happy, because it knew that the carpenter would make him into a treasure chest.

At the second tree the woodsman said, "This looks like a strong tree. I should be able to sell it to the shipyard." The second tree was happy because it knew it was on its way to becoming a mighty ship.

When the woodsman came upon the third tree, the tree was frightened because it knew that if he cut it down its dreams would not come true. The woodsman said, "I don't need anything special from this tree, I'll keep the logs," and he cut it down.

When the first tree arrived at the carpenters, it was made into a feed box for animals. It was then placed in a barn and filled with hay. This was not at all what it had prayed for.

The second tree was cut and made into a small fishing boat. Its dreams of being a mighty ship and carrying kings had come to an end.

The third tree was cut into large pieces, and left alone in the dark.

The years went by, and the trees forgot about their dreams.

Then one day, a man and a woman came to the barn. She gave birth and they placed the baby in the hay in the feed box that was made from the first tree. The man wished that he could have made a crib for the baby, but this manger would have to do. The tree could feel the importance of this event and knew that it had held the greatest treasure of all time.

Years later, a group of men got in the fishing boat made from the second tree. One of them was tired and went to sleep. While they were out on the water, a great storm arose and the tree didn't think it was strong enough to keep the men safe. The men woke the sleeping man, and He stood and said 'Peace' and the storm stopped. At this time, the tree knew that it had carried the King of Kings in its boat.

Finally, someone came and got the third tree. It was carried through the streets as the people mocked the man who was carrying it. When they came to a stop, the man was nailed to the tree and raised in the air to die at the top of a hill. When

Sunday came, the tree came to realize that it was strong enough to stand at the top of the hill and be as close to God as was possible, because Jesus had been crucified on it.

Moral: When things don't seem to be going your way, always know that God has a plan for you. If you place your trust in Him, God will give you great gifts.

Each of the trees got what they wanted, just not in the way they had imagined.

We don't always know what God's plans are for us. We just know that His ways are not our ways, but His ways are always the best.

A poor man asked Buddha, "Why am I so poor?"

Buddha said, "Because you do not learn to give."

The poor man said, "But I'm not having anything?"

Buddha said: "You have a few things ...

The Face, which can give a smile;

The Mouth, which can praise or comfort others;

The Heart, which can open up to others;

The Eyes, which can admire others;

The Body, which can be used to help others."

Self-Improvement

Once there was a crow who lived in a big banyan tree, where a number of peacocks also lived. He saw the beautiful plumes of the peacocks and cherished a desire to look like one of them. He often cursed himself for being ugly. He scorned the whole crow community being black and ugly. He wanted to look like a peacock so that the people may praise him.

In order to fulfil his ambition, he thought of a plan. He decided to collect dropped off feathers of the peacocks and fix them up into his own, so that he may look beautiful like a peacock. After putting on the feathers of the peacock, the crow considered himself to be a peacock. He was full of joy. He decided to go and live with the peacocks.

He took a long flight and reached the place where some peacocks were walking around. He walked up and down among the peacocks. The peacocks saw this strange bird with surprise. It looked half crow and half peacock. The peacocks are known for their self-pride. They could not tolerate a crow posing to be a peacock. At once they pounced upon the crow and broke away some of his artificial feathers.

The crow was able to save his life with great difficulty. He flew at full speed for his life to a place where some crows were perching. He began to move about proudly among the crows. The crows took it to be a different bird, resembling a peacock. They could not tolerate the presence of a peacock among themselves; and attacked him, pecking him hard with their beaks.

Again the crow had to fly away for his life. He was pained at heart and flew to a lonely tree in the jungle. He did not know what to do. He thought, he had tried to improve himself by fixing peacocks' feathers into his own, but they could not make him a peacock. He was not accommodated by the peacocks, rather he was attacked for being an imposter. Not only this, even his own brethren—the crows disowned him.

He was at a loss to know what to do now. At last he tore off all of his peacock feathers and became a crow again. It was only then that the crows owned him as one of them and accommodated him among themselves. The foolish crow had a bitter experience. He learnt a lesson for life—Do not adopt unnatural and unfair methods for self-improvement and do not try to copy others.

> *Once a man had stopped by a river to drink water. There he saw a scorpion floundering around in the water. He decided to save it by stretching out his fingers, but the scorpion stung him. The man still tried to get the scorpion out of the water, but the scorpion stung him again.*
>
> *A man nearby told him to stop saving the scorpion that kept stinging him.*
>
> *But he replied, "It is the nature of the scorpion to sting. It is my nature to love. Why should I give up my nature to love when even the scorpion is not giving up its nature to sting?"*

The Fresh Fish

The Japanese have always loved fresh fish. But the waters close to Japan have not held many fish for decades. So to feed the Japanese population, fishing boats got bigger and went farther than ever. The farther the fishermen went, the longer it took to bring in the fish. If the return trip took more than a few days, the fish did not remain fresh. The Japanese did not like the taste.

To solve this problem, fishing companies installed freezers on their boats. They would catch the fish and freeze them at sea. Freezers allowed the boats to go farther and stay longer. However, the Japanese could taste the difference between fresh and frozen and they did not like frozen fish. The frozen fish brought a lower price. So fishing companies installed fish tanks. They would catch the fish and stuff them in the tanks, fin to fin. After a little thrashing around, the fish stopped moving. They were tired and dull, but alive. Unfortunately, the Japanese could still taste the difference. Because the fish did not move for days, they lost their fresh-fish taste. The Japanese preferred the lively taste of fresh fish, not sluggish fish.

Here is how the Japanese solved this problem. To keep the fish tasting fresh, the Japanese fishing companies still put the fish in the tanks. But now they add a small shark to each tank. The shark eats a few fish, but most of the fish arrive in a very lively state. The fish are challenged!

Have you realized that some of us are also living in a pond but most of the time tired and dull. So we need a shark in our life to keep us awake and moving. Basically in our lives sharks are new challenges to keep us active and lively.

Prayer

Prayer doesn't only happen when we kneel or put hands together and meditate!

When you hug a friend that's a prayer.

When you cook something to nourish family and friends, that's a prayer.

When you send off your near and dear ones and say 'Drive Safely' or 'Be Safe', that's a prayer too.

When you are helping someone in need by giving your time, energy and money, you are praying.

When you wish someone well, you are praying!

Prayer is a vibration.

A feeling.

A thought.

Prayer is the voice of love, friendship and genuine relationships!

Prayer is the best antivirus of world which protects windows of our life from fatal viruses of sorrow, gloom, sin and hopelessness. So update your antivirus daily.

*   *   *

The first ever cordless phone was created by God. He named it "Prayer". It never loses its signal and you never have to recharge it. Use it anywhere!

The Returned Gift

One day Gautam Buddha was walking through a village. A very angry and rude young man came up and began insulting him. "You have no right teaching others," he shouted. "You are as stupid as everyone else. You are nothing but a fake."

Buddha was not upset by these insults. Instead he asked the young man "Tell me, if you buy a gift for someone, and that person does not take it, to whom does the gift belong?"

The man was surprised to be asked such a strange question and answered, "It would belong to me, because I bought the gift."

The Buddha smiled and said, "That is correct. And it is exactly the same with your anger. If you become angry with me and I do not get insulted, then the anger falls back on you. You are then the only one who becomes unhappy, not me. All you have done is hurt yourself."

10% conflicts are due to difference in opinion and 90% are due to wrong tone of voice.

* * *

If you are right then there is no need to get angry, and if you are wrong, then you don't have any right to get angry.

* * *

The only way to have a friend is to be one.

Perfect Action

Delete	→	Sorrow
Save	→	Joy
Recharge	→	Relationship
Download	→	Friendship
Erase	→	Enemosity
Broadcast	→	Truth
Switch Off	→	Lies
Tension	→	Not Reachable
Love	→	Incoming
Hatred	→	Outgoing
Laughter	→	Inbox
Tears	→	Outbox
Anger	→	On Hold
Smile	→	Sent
Help	→	OK
Heart	→	Vibrate

Now you will find the ringtone of your life ringing so melodiously!

If you think Mona Lisa is stunning, you should look at my masterpiece in the mirror. —God

Two Stories

Story Number One

Many years ago, Al Capone virtually owned Chicago. Capone wasn't famous for anything heroic. He was notorious for enmeshing the windy city in everything from bootlegged booze and prostitution to murder.

Capone had a lawyer nicknamed 'Easy Eddie'. He was Capone's lawyer for a good reason. Eddie was very good! In fact, Eddie's skills at legal manoeuvering kept Big Al out of jail for a long time.

To show his appreciation, Capone paid him very well. Not only was the money big, but Eddie got special dividends as well. For instance, he and his family occupied a fenced-in mansion with all the conveniences of the day. The estate was so large that it filled an entire Chicago City block.

Eddie lived the high life of the Chicago mob and gave little consideration to the atrocities that went on around him. Eddie did have one soft spot, however. He had a son that he loved dearly. Eddie saw to it that his son got best of education and everything he desired. Nothing was withheld. Price was no object.

And, despite his involvement with organized crime, Eddie even tried to teach him right from wrong. Eddie wanted his son to be a better man than he was. Yet, with all his wealth and influence, there were two things he couldn't give his son; he couldn't pass on a good name or a good example.

One day, Easy Eddie reached a difficult decision. Easy Eddie wanted to rectify wrongs he had done. He decided he would go to the authorities and tell the truth about Al 'Scarface' Capone, clean up his tarnished name, and offer his son some semblance of integrity. To do this, he would have to testify against the mob, and he knew that the cost would be great. So, he testified.

Within the year, Easy Eddie's life ended in a blaze of gunfire on a lonely Chicago Street. But in his eyes, he had given his son the greatest gift he had to offer, at the greatest price he would ever pay.

Story Number Two

World War II produced many heroes. One such man was Lieutenant Commander Butch O'Hare. He was a fighter pilot assigned to the aircraft carrier Lexington in the South Pacific. One day his entire squadron was sent on a mission. After he was airborne, he looked at his fuel gauge and realized that someone had forgotten to top off his fuel tank. He would not have enough fuel to complete his mission and get back to his ship.

His flight leader told him to return to the carrier. Reluctantly, he dropped out of the formation and headed back to the fleet. As he was returning to the mother ship, he saw something that turned his blood cold; a squadron of Japanese Aircraft was speeding its way towards the American Fleet.

The American fighters were gone on a sortie, and the fleet was all but defenseless. He couldn't reach his squadron and bring them back in time to save the fleet. Nor could he warn the fleet of the approaching danger. There was only one thing to do. He must somehow divert them from the fleet.

Laying aside all thoughts of personal safety, he dove into the formation of Japanese planes. Wing-mounted 50 caliber's blazed as he charged in, attacking one surprised enemy plane and then another. Butch wove in and out of the now broken formation and fired at as many planes as possible until all his ammunition was finally spent.

Undaunted, he continued the assault. He dove at the planes, trying to clip a wing or tail in hope of damaging as many enemy planes as possible, rendering them unfit to fly. Finally, the exasperated Japanese squadron took off in another direction.

Deeply relieved, Butch O'Hare and his tattered fighter limped back to the carrier. Upon arrival, he reported the event surrounding his return. The film from the gun-camera mounted on his plane told the tale. It showed the extent of Butch's daring attempt to protect his fleet. He had, in fact, destroyed five enemy aircraft.

This took place on February 20, 1942, and for that action Butch became the Navy's first Ace of World War II, and the first Naval Aviator to win the Medal of Honor.

A year later Butch was killed in an aerial combat at the age of 29. His home town would not allow the memory of this WW II hero to fade, and today, O'Hare Airport in Chicago is named in tribute to the courage of this great man.

The next time you find yourself at O'Hare International, visit Butch's memorial displaying his statue and his Medal of Honor. It's located between Terminals 1 and 2.

So, what do these two stories have to do with each other?

Butch O'Hare was Easy Eddie's son!

Look for God in others.

How to Stay Young

1. Throw out nonessential numbers. This includes age, weight and height. Let the doctors worry about them. That is why you pay them.

2. Keep only cheerful friends. The grouches pull you down.

3. Keep learning! Learn more about the computer, crafts, gardening, whatever. Never let the brain idle. "An idle mind is the devil's workshop." And the devil's family name is Alzheimer.

4. Laugh often, long and loud. Laugh until you gasp for breath.

5. The tears happen. Endure, grieve, and move on. The only person, who is with us our entire life, is ourselves. Be ALIVE while you are alive.

6. Surround yourself with what you love, whether it's family, pets, music, plants, hobbies, whatever. Your home is your refuge.

7. Cherish your health. If it is good, preserve it. If it is unstable, improve it. If it is beyond what you can improve, get help.

8. Don't take guilt trips. Take a trip to the mall, even to the next county; to a foreign country but NOT to where the guilt is.

9. Tell the people you love that you love them, at every opportunity.

And always remember:

Life is not measured by the number of breaths we take, but by the moments that take our breath away!

A Tale of Two Seas

Sitting in the Geography class in school, I remember how fascinated I was when we were being taught all about the Dead Sea. As you probably recall, the Dead Sea is really a lake, not a sea. It is so high in salt content that the human body can float easily. You can almost lie down and read a book! The salt in the Dead Sea is as high as 35%, almost 10 times the normal ocean water. And all that saltiness has meant that there is no life at all in the Dead Sea. No fish, no vegetation, no sea animals. Nothing lives in the Dead Sea. And hence the name—Dead Sea.

While the Dead Sea has remained etched in my memory, I don't seem to recall learning about the Sea of Galilee in my school Geography lesson. So when I heard about the Sea of Galilee and the Dead Sea and the tale of the two seas—I was intrigued. Turns out that the Sea of Galilee is just north of the Dead Sea. Both the Sea of Galilee and the Dead Sea receive their water from river Jordan. And yet, they are very, very different.

Unlike the Dead Sea, the Sea of Galilee is pretty resplendent with rich colorful marine life. There are lots of plants. And lots of fish too. In fact, the sea of Galilee is home to over twenty different types of fishes.

Same region, same source of water, and yet while one sea is full of life, the other is dead. How come?

Here apparently is why. The River Jordan flows into the Sea of Galilee and then flows out. The water simply passes through the Sea of Galilee, in and then out, and that keeps the Sea healthy and vibrant, teeming with marine life.

But the Dead Sea is so far below the mean sea level, that it has no outlet. The water flows in from the river Jordan, but does not flow out. There are no outlet streams. It is estimated that over a million tons of water evaporate from the Dead Sea every day. Leaving it salty. Too full of minerals. And unfit for any marine life.

The Dead Sea takes water from the River Jordan, and holds it. It does not give. Result? No life at all. Think about it.

Life is not just about getting/acquiring. Its about giving/sharing. We all need to be a bit like the Sea of Galilee.

We are fortunate to have wealth, knowledge, love and respect. But if we do not learn to give, we could all end up like the Dead Sea. The love and the respect, the wealth, beauty and the knowledge could all evaporate with time. Just like the water of the Dead Sea.

If we get the Dead Sea mentality of merely taking in more water, more money, more of everything; the result can be disastrous. It will be a good idea to make sure that in the sea of your own life, you must have outlets. Many outlets. For love and for wealth, and everything else that you get in your life. Make sure you don't just keep it to yourself, you must give it away too. Open the taps of your mind. And you'll open the floodgates to happiness.

> *A good heart can win many relationships,*
> *A good nature can win many good hearts!*
>
> *   *   *
>
> *Treat everyone with politeness, even those who are rude to you. Not because they are not nice, but because you are nice.*

Dirty Laundry

A young couple moved into a new neighbourhood. The next morning while they were eating breakfast, the young woman saw her neighbour hanging the laundry outside. "The laundry is not very clean." She said. "She doesn't know how to wash properly, perhaps she needs better laundry soap."

Her husband looked on but remained silent. Every time her neighbour would hang her clothes to dry, the young woman would make the same comment.

About one month later, the woman was surprised to see a nice clean wash on the line and said to her husband: "Look, she has learned how to wash properly. I wonder who taught her this."

The husband said: "I got up early this morning and cleaned our windows."

And so it is with life. What we see when watching others depends on the purity of the window through which we look!!!

A wise man once sat in the audience and cracked a joke. All laughed like crazy. After a moment he cracked the same joke again and a little less people laughed this time. He cracked the same joke again and again. When there was no laughter in the crowd, he smiled and said, "When you can't laugh on the same joke again and again, then why do you keep crying over the same thing over and over again. So forget the past and move on.

Fifteen Things to Give Up

Here is a list of 15 things, which, if you give up, will make your life a lot easier and you'll feel much happier. We hold on to so many things that cause us a great deal of pain, stress and suffering and instead of letting them all go and allowing ourselves to be stress-free and happy, we cling on to them.

Well, not anymore. Starting today, we will give up on all those things that no longer serve us, and will embrace change. Ready? Here we go!

1. **Give up your need to always be right.** There are so many of us who can't stand the idea of being wrong, wanting to always be right even at the risk of ending great relationships or causing a great deal of stress and pain for us and for others. It's just not worth it.

2. **Give up your need for control.** Be willing to give up your need to always control everything that happens to you and around you—situations, events, people, etc. Whether they are loved ones, co-workers, or just strangers you meet on the street, just allow them to be just as they are and you will see how much better will that make you feel.

3. **Give up on blame.** Give up on your need to blame others for what you have or don't have, for what you feel or don't feel. Start taking responsibility for your life.

4. **Give up your self-defeating self-talk.** How many people are hurting themselves because of their negative, polluted and repetitive self-defeating mindset. Don't believe everything that your mind is telling you, especially if it's negative and self-defeating.

5. **Give up your limiting beliefs about what you can or cannot do, about what is possible or impossible.** From now on, you are no longer going to allow your limiting beliefs to keep you stuck. Spread your wings and fly! A belief is not an idea held by the mind, it is an idea that holds the mind.

6. **Give up complaining.** Give up your constant need to complain about those things, people, situations and events that make you unhappy, sad and depressed. Nobody can make you unhappy, no situation can make you sad or miserable unless you allow it to. It's not the situation that triggers those feelings in you, but how you choose to look at it. Never underestimate the power of positive thinking.

7. **Give up the luxury of criticism.** Give up your need to criticize things, events or people that are different than you. We are all different, yet we are all the same. We all want to be happy, we all want to love and be loved and we all want to be understood.

8. **Give up your need to impress others.** Stop trying to be something that you're not, just to make others admire you. It doesn't work this way. The moment you stop trying to be something that you're not, you take off all your masks, you accept and embrace the real you, you will find people will be drawn to you effortlessly.

9. **Give up your resistance to change.** Change is good. Change will help you make improvements in your life and also the lives of those around you. Embrace change, don't resist it and the universe will open doors for you where there were only walls.

10. **Give up labels.** Stop labeling things, people or events that you don't understand as being weird or different and try opening your mind. Minds work best when open.

11. **Give up on your fears.** Fear is just an illusion, it doesn't exist, you created it. It's all in your mind. Correct the inside and the outside will fall into place.

12. **Give up your excuses.** A lot of times we limit ourselves because of the many excuses we use. Instead of growing and working on improving ourselves and our lives, we get stuck and lie to ourselves, using all kinds of excuses. Excuses that 99.9% of the time are not even real.

13. **Give up the past.** This one's hard. Especially when the past looks so much better than the present and the future looks so frightening. But you have to take into consideration the fact that the present moment is all you have and all you will ever have. Be present in everything you do and enjoy life. After all, life is a journey, not a destination. Have a clear vision for the future, prepare yourself, but always live the present moment to its fullest.

14. **Give up attachment.** This is a concept that, for most of us, is so hard to grasp, but it's not impossible. The moment you detach yourself from all things, you become so peaceful, so tolerant, so kind, and so serene. You will attain a mindset where you will be able to understand all things without even trying. A state beyond words.

15. **Give up living your life to other people's expectations.** Way too many people are living a life that is not theirs to live. They live their lives according to what others think is best for them. They ignore their inner voice, that inner calling. They are so busy with pleasing everybody, with living up to other people's expectations, that they lose control over their lives. They forget what makes them happy, what they want, what they need and eventually, they forget about themselves. You have one life. Live to its fullest each day!

Team Work

A man was lost while driving through the countryside. As he tried to reach for the map, he accidentally drove off the road into a ditch. Though he wasn't injured, his car was stuck deep in the mud. So the man walked to a nearby farm to ask for help.

"Badal can get you out of that ditch," said the farmer, pointing to a horse standing in a field.

The man looked at the horse and looked at the farmer who just stood there repeating, "Yes, old Badal can do the job."

The man figured he had nothing to lose. The two men and the horse made their way back to the ditch. The farmer hitched the horse to the car. With a snap of the reins, he shouted, "Pull, Bhola! Pull, Moti! Pull, Hira! Pull, Badal!"

And Badal pulled that car right out of the ditch. The man was amazed. He thanked the farmer, patted the horse, and asked, "Why did you call out all those names before you called Badal?"

The farmer grinned and said, "Old Badal is blind. As long as he believes he's part of a team, he doesn't mind pulling."

Alone we can do so little;

Together we can do so much.

—Hellen Keller

Shoe Maker

On his first day in office, as President Abraham Lincoln entered to give his inaugural address, one man stood up. He was a rich Aristocrat. He Said, "Mr. Lincoln, you should not forget that your father used to make shoes for my family."

And the whole Senate laughed. They thought they had made a fool of Lincoln. But certain people are made of a totally different mettle.

Lincoln looked at the man directly in the eyes and said, "Sir, I know that my father used to make shoes for your family, and there will be many others here, because he made shoes the way nobody else can. He was a creator. His shoes were not just shoes. He poured his whole soul into them. I want to ask you, have you any complain? Because I know how to make shoes myself. If you have any complain, I can make you another pair of shoes. But as far as I know, nobody has ever complained about my father's shoes. He was a genius, a great creator, and I am proud of my father."

The whole Senate was struck dumb. They could not understand what kind of man Abraham Lincoln was. He was proud because his father did his job so well that not even a single complain had ever been heard.

Remember

No one can hurt us without our consent. It is not what happens to us that hurts us. It is our response that hurts us.

Advice to 50+ Years Old

Because none of us have many years to live, and we can't take along anything when we go, so we don't have to be too thrifty.

Spend the money that should be spent, enjoy what should be enjoyed, donate what you are able to donate, but don't leave all to your children or grandchildren, for you don't want them to become parasites who are waiting for the day you will die!

Don't worry about what will happen after we are gone, because when we return to dust, we will feel nothing about praises or criticisms. The time to enjoy the worldly life and your hard earned wealth will be over.

Don't worry too much about your children, for children will have their own destiny and should find their own way. Don't be your children's slave. Care for them, love them, give them gifts but also enjoy your money while you can. Life should have more to it than working from the cradle to the grave.

Don't expect too much from your children. Caring children, though caring, would be too busy with their jobs and commitments to render much help. Uncaring children may fight over your assets even when you are still alive, and wish for your early demise so they can inherit your properties and wealth.

50-year old like you, don't trade in your health for wealth by working yourself to an early grave anymore. Because your money may not be able to buy you health.

When to stop making money, and how much is enough?

Out of thousand hectares of good farm land, you can consume only less than a kg of rice daily; out of a thousand mansions, you only need eight square meters of space to rest at night. So, as long as you have enough food and enough money to spend, that is good enough.

You should live happily. Every family has its own problems. Just do not compare with others for fame and social status and see whose children are doing better, etc., but challenge others for happiness, health, enjoyment, quality of life and longevity.

Don't worry about things that you can't change because it doesn't help and it may spoil your health. You have to create your own well-being and find your own place of happiness. As long as you are in good mood and good health, think about happy things, do happy things daily and have fun in doing, then you will pass your time happily every day. One day passes without happiness, you will lose one day. One day passes with happiness, and then you gain one day.

In a good spirit, sickness will cure; in a happy spirit, sickness will cure faster; in high and happy spirits, sickness will never come.

With good mood, suitable amount of exercise, always in the sun, variety of foods, reasonable amount of vitamin and mineral intake, hopefully you will live another 30 or 40 years of healthy life of pleasure.

Above all, learn to treasure your friends, they all make you feel young and 'wanted'. Without them you are surely to feel lost!!!

Worry is like a rocking chair.

It gives you something to do, but gets you nowhere.

Perfection

A German once visited a temple under construction where he saw a sculptor making an idol of God. He noticed a similar idol lying nearby. Surprised, he asked the sculptor, "Do you need two statues of the same idol?"

"No," said the sculptor without looking up, "We need only one, but the first one got damaged at the last stage."

The gentleman examined the idol and found no apparent damage. "Where is the damage?" He asked.

"There is a scratch on the nose of the idol." Said the sculptor, still busy with his work.

"Where are you going to install the idol?"

The sculptor replied that it would be installed on a pillar twenty feet high.

"If the idol is that far, who is going to know that there is a scratch on the nose?" The gentleman asked.

The sculptor stopped his work, looked up at the gentleman, smiled and said, "I will know it."

Perfection is not attainable, but if we chase perfection we can catch excellence.

*   *   *

Husband to Wife: You should learn to embrace your mistakes.
She hugged him tightly.

Courtesies

I ran into a stranger as he passed by,
"Oh excuse me please" was my reply.
He said, "Please excuse me too,
I wasn't watching for you."
We were very polite, this stranger and I.
We went on our way and we said goodbye.
But at home a different story is told,
How we treat our loved ones, young and old.

Later that day, cooking the evening meal,
My son stood beside me very still.
When I turned, I nearly knocked him down,
"Move out of the way," I said with a frown.
He walked away, his little heart broken,
I didn't realize how harshly I'd spoken.

While I lay awake in bed,
God's still small voice came to me and said,
"While dealing with a stranger,
common courtesy you use,
but the family you love, you seem to abuse.
Go and look on the kitchen floor,
You'll find some flowers there by the door.
Those are the flowers he brought for you,
He picked them himself: pink, yellow and blue.
He stood very quietly not to spoil the surprise,
you never saw the tears that filled his little eyes."

By this time, I felt very small,
And now my tears began to fall.
I quietly went and knelt by his bed;
"Wake up, little one, wake up," I said.
"Are these the flowers you picked for me?"
He smiled, "I found them out by the tree.
I picked them because they're pretty like you.
I knew you'd like them, especially the blue."

I said, "Son, I'm very sorry for the way I acted today,
I shouldn't have yelled at you that way."
He said, "Oh, Mom, that's okay, I love you any way."
I said, "Son, I love you too,
and I do like the flowers, especially the blue."

Beginning today, treat everyone you meet as if they were going to be dead by midnight. Extend to them all the care, kindness and understanding you can muster, and do it with no thought of any reward. Your life will never be the same again.

*   *   *

Success is like a beautiful lover
It will leave us at anytime,
But failure is like a mother
It will teach us some important lessons of life!

Acceptance

A man and his girlfriend got married. It was a huge celebration. All of their friends and family came to see the lovely ceremony and to partake of the festivities and celebrations. A wonderful time was had by all.

The bride was gorgeous in her wedding attire and the groom was very dashing in his *sherwani*. Everyone could tell that the love they had for each other was true.

A few months later, the wife comes to the husband with a proposal: "I read in a magazine, a while ago, about how we can strengthen our marriage. Each of us will write a list of things that we find a bit annoying with the other person. Then, we can talk about how we can fix them together and make our lives happier."

The husband agreed, so each of them went to a separate room in the house and thought of the things that annoyed them about the other. They thought about this question for the rest of the day and wrote down what they came up with.

The next morning, at the breakfast table, they decided that they would go over their lists. "I'll start," offered the wife. She took out her list. It had many items on it which filled three pages. As she started reading the list of the little annoyances, she noticed that tears were starting to appear in her husband's eyes. "What's wrong?" She asked.

"Nothing", the husband replied, "Keep reading your list."

The wife continued to read until she had read all three pages to her husband.

"Now, you read your list and then we'll talk about the things on both of our lists." She said happily.

Quietly the husband stated, "I don't have anything on my list. I think that you are perfect the way you are. I don't want you to change anything for me. You are lovely and wonderful and I wouldn't want to try and change anything about you."

The wife, touched by the depth of his love for her and his acceptance of her, turned her head and wept.

If a drop of water falls in a lake, its identity is lost.
BUT
If a drop of water falls on a lotus leaf, it shines like a pearl.
Drop is the same,
but the 'COMPANY' matters.

      *   *   *

Always take extra care of three things in your life!
TRUST,
PROMISE
&
RELATIONSHIP!
They don't make noise when they break,
they only create SILENCE in Life....!

Making a Difference

A man was walking down a deserted beach at sunset. As he walked along he began to see another man in the distance.

As he grew nearer he noticed that the local native kept leaning down, picking something up, and throwing it into the water. Time and again he kept hurling things out into the ocean.

As our friend approached even closer he noticed that the man was picking up starfish that had washed up onto the beach, and one at a time, he was throwing them back into the ocean.

The first man was puzzled. He approached the man and said, "Good evening, friend, I was wondering what are you doing?" And he replied, "I'm throwing these starfish back into the ocean. You see, it's low tide right now and all these starfish have been washed up onto the shore. If I don't throw them back into the sea, they will die."

"I understand," my friend replied "but there must be thousands of starfish on this beach and you couldn't possibly get to all of them. There are simply too many and don't you realize that this is happening on hundreds of beaches up and down this coast ... can't you see that you can't possibly make a difference?

The local native smiled, bent down, picked up yet another starfish ... and as he threw it back out into the sea, he replied, "It made a difference to that one!"

> *Great opportunities to help others seldom come, but small ones surround us every day.*

Start Over

When you've trusted God and walked His way
When you've felt His hand lead you day by day
But your steps now take you another way...
START OVER!

When you've made your plans and they've gone awry
When you've tried your best and there's no more try
When you've failed yourself and you don't know why...
START OVER!

When you've told your friends what you plan to do
When you've trusted them and they didn't come through
And you're all alone and it's up to you...
START OVER!

When you've failed your kids and they're grown and gone
When you've done your best but it's turned out wrong
And now your grandchildren come along...
START OVER!

When you've prayed to God so you'll know His will
When you've prayed and prayed and you don't know still
When you want to stop because you've had your fill...
START OVER!

The Seed Story

An emperor was growing old and knew it was time to choose his successor. Instead of choosing one of his assistants or his children, he decided something different. He called young people in the kingdom together one day. He said, "It is time for me to step down and choose the next emperor. I have decided to choose one of you."

The kids were shocked! But the emperor continued, "I am going to give each one of you a seed today. One very special seed. I want you to plant the seed, water it and come back here one year from today with what you have grown from this one seed. I will then judge the plants that you bring, and the owner of the one I choose will be the next emperor!"

A boy named Aryavir was there that day and he, like others, received a seed. He went home and excitedly told his mother the story. She helped him get a pot and planting soil, and he planted the seed and watered it carefully. Every day he would water it and watch to see if it had grown. After about three weeks, some of the other youths began to talk about their seeds and the plants that were beginning to grow.

Aryavir kept checking his seed, but nothing ever grew. Three weeks, 4 weeks, 5 weeks went by. Still nothing. By now, others were talking about their plants but Aryavir didn't have a plant, and he felt like a failure. Six months went by—still nothing in Aryavir's pot. He just knew he had killed his seed. Everyone else had trees and tall plants, but he had nothing. Aryavir didn't say anything to his friends, however. He just kept waiting for his seed to grow.

The year finally went by and all the youths of the kingdom brought their plants to the emperor for inspection. Aryavir told his mother that he wasn't going to take an empty pot. But honest about what had happened, his mother advised him to at least go and admit his defeat. He knew his mother was right. He took his empty pot to the palace. When Aryavir arrived, he was amazed at the variety of plants grown by the other youths. They were beautiful—in all shapes and sizes. Aryavir put his empty pot on the floor and many other kids laughed at him.

When the emperor arrived, he surveyed the room and greeted the young people. Aryavir just tried to hide in the back. "My, what great plants, trees and flowers you have grown," said the emperor. "Today, one of you will be appointed the next emperor!" All of a sudden, the emperor spotted Aryavir at the back of the room with his empty pot. He ordered his guards to bring him to the front. Aryavir was terrified. "The emperor knows I'm a failure. Maybe he will have me killed."

When Aryavir got to the front, the Emperor asked his name. "My name is Aryavir" he replied. All the kids were laughing and making fun of him. The emperor asked everyone to quiet down. He looked at Aryavir, and then announced to the crowd, "Behold your new emperor! His name is Aryavir!" Aryavir couldn't believe it. He couldn't even grow his seed. How could he be the new emperor? Then the emperor said, "One year ago this day, I gave everyone here a seed. I told you to take the seed, plant it, water it, and bring it back to me today. But I gave you all boiled seeds which would not grow. All of you, except Aryavir, have brought me trees and plants and flowers. When you found that the seed would not grow, you substituted another seed for the one I gave you. Aryavir was the only one with the courage and honesty to bring me a pot with my seed in it. Therefore, he is the one who will be the new emperor!"

Plant with Care

If you plant honesty, You will reap trust

If you plant goodness, You will reap friends

If you plant humility, You will reap greatness

If you plant perseverance, You will reap victory

If you plant hard work, You will reap success

If you plant forgiveness, You will reap reconciliation

If you plant faith, You will reap miracles.

But

If you plant dishonesty, You will reap distrust

If you plant selfishness, You will reap loneliness

If you plant envy, You will reap trouble

If you plant laziness, You will reap stagnation

If you plant greed, You will reap loss

If you plant gossip, You will reap enemies

If you plant worries, You will reap wrinkles.

So be careful what you plant now, it will determine what you will reap tomorrow. The seeds you now scatter, will make life worse or better. Some day, you will enjoy the fruits, or you will pay for the choices you plant today.

Seasons

There was a man who had four sons. He wanted his sons to learn not to Judge things too quickly. So he sent them each on a quest, in turns, to go and look at a pear tree that was a great distance away.

The first son went in the winter, the second in the spring, the third in summer, and the youngest son in the fall. When they had all gone and come back, he called them together to describe what they had seen.

The first son said that the tree was ugly, bent and twisted. The second son said, no, it was covered with green buds and full of promise. The third son disagreed; he said it was laden with blossoms that smelled so sweet and looked so beautiful, it was the most graceful thing he had ever seen. The last son disagreed with all of them; he said it was ripe and drooping with fruits, full of life and fulfillment.

The man then explained to his sons that they were all right, because they had each seen but only one season in the tree's life. He told them that you cannot judge a tree, or a person, by only one season, and that the essence of who they are and the pleasure, joy and love that comes can only be measured at the end, when all the seasons are up.

If you give up when it's winter, you will miss the promise of your spring, the beauty of your summer, fulfillment of your fall. Don't let the pain of one season destroy the joy of all the rest. Don't judge life by one difficult season. Persevere through the difficult patches and better times are sure to come some time.

Follow Your Dream

I will tell you a story of my friend Udit. When he was a kid, his father as a horse trainer used to move from stable to stable, from ranch to ranch, training horses. Thus, the boy's school career was constantly interrupted. One day, his teacher asked the class to write about what they wanted to be when they grew up. Udit did not hesitate a minute and wrote a seven-page essay about his aim to be an owner of a horse ranch. He wrote many details and drew a location of buildings and stables and even a detailed house plan.

Two days later he received his paper back with letter "F" on the front page. After class he went to the teacher and asked: "Why did I receive an F?" The teacher responded: "This dream is so unrealistic for a boy like you, who has no money, no resources and who comes from a poor family. There is no possibility that you will reach your great goal one day." Then the teacher asked him to rewrite the paper with more realistic attitude.

The boy went home and asked his father, how should he act. The father answered: "This decision is very important for you. So you have to make your own mind on this."

After several days the boy brought the same paper to his teacher. No changes were made. He said: "Keep the 'F' and I will keep my dream."

Now Udit owns 4,000-square-feet house in the middle of 200-acre horse ranch and he still has that school paper, which now is framed over the fireplace.

The Right Solution

Once the peaceful inhabitants asked one very powerful wizard to stop all wars and bloodshed on the planet.

"It is simple", he said, "I will destroy all weapons on the Earth, and nobody will be able to fight any more."

"It would be fine!" People exclaimed.

The wizard waved the magic wand, and this was done. There was peace on the planet for three days, while the majority of those who were prone to fight, could not find any weapon.

And when they understood they've lost it forever, they contrived spears of young trees, and started to fight again.

When the wizard heard such bad news, he said: "Do not worry. I will destroy all young trees, and these bullies will not be able to fight."

After two or three days of fruitless searching for young trees, suitable for making spears, rebellious people started to cut giant trees, make batons from them, and the blood-shed started again. The Wizard destroyed all big trees.

Then humans made knives and swords of metal. He destroyed all metal on the planet. People made slings and began to throw stones at each other. It was necessary to destroy the stones, too.

And then peacekeepers sounded the alarm: "All trees have disappeared; there is no metal and stones. How to live, what to eat now? There will be no vegetation soon, and people will die without even fighting. No, this is a wrong solution to the problem."

The Wizard became confused: "I do not know what to do now. I would have destroyed all humanity, but, unfortunately, it is not in my power!"

Peacekeepers fell into despair; they did not know what to do. And then one clever kid turned to the Wizard. "I know what you should do. Let people feel, how others perceive their actions. If one person hurts someone, let him feel the same pain, and if he brings joy to someone, let him feel the same joy. So no one will hurt each other, because he will feel pain immediately too, and would have to stop.

All people were inspired with the greatness of the boy's thought, and the wizard embodied his idea exactly. He returned all trees, stones and metals.

Since that day, no one on the planet tried to hurt his neighbour, because he would have to feel the same pain. People began to help each other, because they liked the sense of joy they felt at that moment. And they began to live in harmony and joy.

Your 'Kindness' may be treated as your weakness, "Still be Kind."

Your help to others may go unheeded and unnoticed, "Still be Helpful."

If you are 'Honest' and 'Frank', people may cheat you, "Still be Honest."

The 'Good' you do today, people will often forget tomorrow, "Do Good Anyways."

Because it is between You and GOD.

It was never between you and them.

Making of a Woman

One day, Adam came to God asking to create a partner for him, because he was tired of loneliness. After considering it, God decided to create a Woman and wished to create her wise and harmonious. And then God decided to do this:

He took a little bit of gentleness and tenderness from the morning dew and added there a little bit of strength and stiffness from the rocks which formed the mountains.

Later he took a little bit of assertiveness from the water flow and a bit of flexibility and pliability from the clay, a bit of kingship from the lioness and a little of meekness from the dove, a little bit of kindness and warmth from the evening sun.

He took equal parts of endurance of the ox and fragility of a wildflower, the mystery of the night and the clarity of the day, he added to his masterpiece a little bit from the twitter of the birds and from the silence of the celestial heights.

He wanted to add some other qualities, but he changed His mind. He decided to leave an empty space for creativity of the Spirit. For the last strokes God gave His masterpiece two talents—to be a good mother to her children and a good wife to her husband.

By putting all of these qualities together in a Woman God breathed life into her. So the Woman, spirited and full of Life, stood before God as he created her in the fullness of herself. She wished to look at herself immediately, that is why she glanced at her reflection in the water of the lake and smiled because so beautiful was her appearance!

Limitations

Here's a story about George Dantzig, the famous mathematician, whose contributions to Operations Research and Systems Engineering have made him immortal.

As a college student, George studied very hard, often late into the night, so late, that he overslept one morning, arriving 20 minutes late for Prof. Neyman's class.

He quickly copied the two math's problems on the board, assuming they were the homework assignment. It took him several hours to work through the two problems, but finally he had a breakthrough and dropped the homework on Professor's desk the next day.

Six weeks later, on a Sunday morning, his excited professor awakened George at 6 a.m.

Since George was late for class, he hadn't heard the professor announce that the two unsolvable equations on the board were mathematical mind-teasers that even Einstein hadn't been able to answer!

But George Dantzig, working without any thoughts of limitation, had solved not one, but two problems that had stumped mathematicians for thousands of years.

He simply said, "George solved the problems because he didn't know he couldn't."

> *A person is limited only by the thoughts that he/she chooses.*

Choices

My friend Anup was one of the most positive people I had ever known. He was always in a good mood and always had something encouraging to say.

He was a manager at a restaurant. If his employee had a bad day, Anup always helped him to look at the positive side of the situation.

Anup's attitude truly amazed me. So one day I asked him: "How can you be so positive all the time?" He replied: "You see, every morning I tell myself, that I have two choices for that day—to be in a good mood or in a bad. I choose the good one. And when something wrong happens, I can be sad and angry or I can learn from it instead. I choose to learn. Thus I choose the positive side of life." I said: "It is not that easy." He replied: "Yes it is. Life is all about choices. You can choose how people or situation will affect your mood and your life."

One morning Anup left the restaurant's back door open and was held up at gunpoint by three armed robbers. He tried to open the safe, but his hands shaked due to nervousness and he slipped off the combination. So the robbers shot him. Fortunately, Anup was quickly found and brought to the nearest hospital. After many hours of surgery and long intensive care, Anup was released home.

When I met him, I asked, what were his thoughts during the robbery. "I thought that I should have locked the back door", he replied. "Then, when I was lying on the floor, I remembered about my choices in this case: a choice to live or a choice to die. I chose to live."

I asked, if he was scared. Anup continued: "When they wheeled me into the emergency room and I looked at the faces of doctors, I got truly scared. I knew that I need to do something. So when the nurse asked me if I was allergic to anything, I replied "Yes". Doctors and nurses stopped working and waited for my answer. I took a deep breath and yelled "Bullets". They started laughing and I asked: "My choice is to live, operate me as I am alive, not dead."

Now Anup is alive owing to skills of his doctors, however his amazing attitude played an important role too. I learned from him, that every day we should choose to live fully, no matter what.

> *There is a voice inside of you*
>
> *That whispers all day long,*
>
> *"I feel this is right for me,*
>
> *I know that this is wrong."*
>
> *No teacher, preacher, parent, friend*
>
> *Or wiseman can decide*
>
> *What's that is wrong for you*
>
> *And what is it that is right*
>
> *Just listen to the voice*
>
> *That speaks inside.*

Sharpen Your Skills

Once two woodcutters argued, who of them can cut more wood in eight hours.

In the morning both of them took up their positions. First they worked at the same speed. But after an hour, one of them found that the other one had stopped cutting trees. Realizing that this was his chance, the first woodcutter started to cut trees with double vigour.

Ten minutes passed, and he heard that the second woodcutter started to work again. They were working almost synchronously, when the first woodcutter heard that his opponent had stopped again. The first woodcutter continued to work, feeling the smell of victory.

This lasted all day long. Each hour the second woodcutter stopped for ten minutes and the other one continued to work. When time finished, the first woodcutter who had worked without stopping was absolutely sure that he had won the challenge.

He was very surprised to know that he was mistaken.

"How did that happen?" He asked his opponent, "After each hour I heard that you had stopped work for ten minutes. How could you cut more trees than me? It's impossible!"

"It was very simple", replied the second woodcutter, "After every hour I stopped work for ten minutes. And when you were cutting the trees, in those 10 minutes I sharpened my ax."

The Knots Prayer

Dear God
Please untie the knots
that are in my mind,
my heart and my life.

Remove the have *nots*,
the can *nots* and the do *nots*
that I have in my mind.

Erase the will *nots*,
may *nots*,
might *nots* that may find
a home in my heart.

Release me from the could *nots*,
would *nots* and
should *nots* that obstruct my life.

And most of all,
Dear God,
I ask that you remove from my mind,
my heart and my life all the 'am *nots*'
that I have allowed to hold me back,
especially the thought
that I am *not* good enough.

Amen!

No Rush

Nowadays, there's a movement in Europe named 'Slow Food'. This movement advocates that people should eat and drink slowly, with enough time to taste their food, spend time with family and friends, without rushing. Basically, the movement questions the sense of 'hurry' and 'craziness'.

French people, even though they work 35 hours per week, are more productive than Americans or British, who work more than 40 hours per week. Germans have established 30 hour workweeks and have seen their productivity driven up by 20%. This no-rush attitude doesn't represent doing less or having a lower productivity. It means working and doing things with greater quality, productivity, perfection, with attention to detail and less stress. It means re-establishing family values, friends, free and leisure time.

It means taking humans' essential values, the simplicity of living. It stands for a less coercive work environment, more happy, lighter and more productive work place where humans enjoy doing what they know best how to do.

In the movie, 'Scent of a Woman', there's a scene where Al Pacino asks a girl to dance and she replies, "I can't, my boyfriend will be here any minute now". To which Al Pacino responds, "A life is lived in an instant." Then they dance the tango!

We all have equal time throughout the world. No one has more, or less. The difference lies in how each one of us spend our time. We need to live each moment. As John Lennon said, "Life is what happens to you while you're busy making other plans."

Be Thankful

1. Be thankful that you don't already have everything you desire. If you did, then what would there be to look forward to?

2. Be thankful when you don't know something, for it gives you the opportunity to learn.

3. Be thankful for the difficult times. During those times you grow.

4. Be thankful to your limitations, because they give you opportunities for improvement.

5. Be thankful for each new challenge, because it will build your strength and character.

6. Be thankful for your mistakes. They will teach you valuable lessons.

7. Be thankful when you're tired and weary, because it means you've made an effort.

It is easy to be thankful for the good things. A life of rich fulfillment comes to those who are also thankful for the setbacks. Gratitude can turn a negative into a positive. Find a way to be thankful for your troubles, and they can become you blessings.

> *When GOD solves your problems, you have faith in HIS abilities; when GOD doesn't solve your problems, HE has faith in your abilities.*

Little Things

It was middle of the night and she stirred from her sleep,
She quietly got out of bed and did not make a beep.
She sits in total darkness now and thinks about her man,
The little things he does for her to lend a helping hand.

He helps her all round the house and never makes a mess,
He says it gives her extra time and her work will be less.
She loves him for his thoughtfulness, he does it on his own,
He says he wants to make sure that she never has to moan.

He says, it's really easy and he says he'll never fail,
And promised her that he would never, ever leave a trail.
He said his mother taught him not to clutter all his life,
She also told him, "Don't you ever do it to your wife!"

She has benefited, from a son who was well taught,
All those little things, just magnify his love, she thought.
She loved him from the day they met and loves him more each day,
All the little extra things, sure help along the way.

She sits and thinks of things, that many overlook,
Like cleaning his own coffee cup and hanging it on the hook.
Or when he snacks on party night with friends who have all come,
When it's over and they leave, there's not one single crumb.

She loves him so much for the way, he shows his love to her,
There is no doubt how much he loves her, this she knows for sure.
And she can't help but love his ways, and her love grows for him,
And he won't change his little things, it's how he's always been.

She loves his thoughtfulness for her, and this is one of them,
She thinks while sitting in the darkness, half asleep again.
It's just a little something that, to some may bring a frown,
But the man, she so adores, makes her life like a crown!

Perceptions

It was a beautiful night. Poets lay awake, drawing inspiration from the star spangled sky. Lovers drew closer, gazing at the moon. The elderly came out to feel the cool breeze. Children were playing in the moonlight.

One man watched all this with increasing despair. He was a thief. If nobody slept, how was he to do what he wanted to do? The entire community was awake. He waited endlessly. Somehow the people of this town were just not sleepy that night. Hours of waiting and strolling around in search of a dark sleeping household made the thief very tired. As the night gave way to dawn, he lay down under a tree and within seconds, he was fast asleep.

Even the sun's sharp rays failed to rouse the thief from his deep sleep. A drunkard tottered along and seeing the man lying curled up beneath the tree he muttered: "This guy must be my master. He must have drunk so much that he is still not able to get up. Stupid fellow doesn't know his limits..." Another passerby, a professional gambler, stopped and bent down to check the sleeping man's pockets. Finding them empty, he checked his own and was satisfied that his cash was safe. "Poor guy!" He thought to himself, "He must have gambled all night to his last paisa. Too bad he didn't know when to stop. His wife wouldn't have let him in the house and so the poor fellow must have fallen asleep here."

The day was gathering momentum. The sun was really sharp and yet the thief was asleep. A few schoolchildren were playing football. A passerby cautioned them, "Look children, there is a man sleeping here. Be careful not to disturb him." Having advised the children the man who was also a thief went closer to the sleeping man. "He must be a thief like me who having found nothing all night is trying to sleep off his frustration."

The greatest truth is that a single person or fact can be looked at in many different ways. We saw how one sleeping man evoked so many different reactions. Similarly, any one incident or utterance can be interpreted to mean very many different things. To be able to accept the possibility those other perceptions may also be true or plausible is the philosophy of *anekta*.

When you go into a garden and see different kinds of flowers in full bloom, you marvel at nature and enjoy the beauty of each flower, its unique shape, colour and perfume. But when you walk into a room full of people, each holding a view different from yours, you find it difficult to accept. A positive attitude will make you grow. You will be able to achieve happiness and spread it around, making the world a better place to live in.

Journey of Life starts with full bag of Luck and empty bag of Experience.

The Goal is to fill the bag of Experience,

before the bag of Luck gets empty.

*   *   *

We ourselves feel that what we are doing is just a drop in the ocean. But the ocean would be less because of that missing drop.

Woman

You can feel her care in form of a sister.

You can feel her warmth in form of a friend.

You can feel her passion in form of a beloved.

You can feel her dedication in form of a wife.

You can feel her divinity in form of a mother.

You can feel her blessings in form of a grandmother.

She is tough, tender hearted, naughty, charming, sharing and caring.

She is a woman.

She is life!

Do you know, why God created gaps between fingers?

So that someone who is special to you, comes and fills those gaps by holding your hands forever.

* * *

Search a beautiful heart not a beautiful face.

Beautiful things are not always good

but good things are always beautiful.

Situation Vacant

Staff wanted urgently for the following SIX vacancies:

1. An ELECTRICIAN
   ...to restore the current between people who do not speak to each other anymore.

2. An OPTICIAN
   ...to change the outlook of people.

3. An ARTIST
   ...to draw a smile on everyone's face.

4. A CONSTRUCTION WORKER
   ...to build peace.

5. A GARDENER
   ...to cultivate good thoughts.

And

6. A MATH TEACHER
   ...to teach us how to count on each other.

> *Relationships—of all kinds—are like sand held in your hand. Held loosely, with an open hand, the sand remains where it is. The minute you close your hand and squeeze tightly to hold on, the sand trickles through your fingers. You may hold on to some of it, but most will be spilled. A relationship is like that; hold loosely, with respect and freedom for the other person, it is likely to remain intact. But hold too tightly, too possessively, and the relationship slips away and is lost.*

Now, Instead

When I'll be dead
your tears will flow,
but I won't know.
Cry for me now, instead!

You will send flowers
but I won't see.
Send them now, instead!

You will say words of praise
but I won't hear.
Praise me now, instead!

You will forget my faults
but I won't know.
Forget them now, instead!

You will miss me then
but I won't feel.
Miss me now, instead!

You will wish you could have
spent more time with me.
Spend it now, instead!

God has Fallen in Love with You

He sends you flowers every spring.

He sends you sunshine every morning.

Whenever you want to talk, he listens to you.

He can live anywhere in the universe, and yet he chooses to live in YOUR HEART.

Let's face it, He is crazy about you!!!

God did not promise

   days without pain,

   laughter without sorrow,

   sun without rain.

But he did promise

   strength for the day,

   comfort for the tears, and

   light for the way!

Whenever you share the goodness in your heart,

you always end up WINNING,

because LIFE is an ECHO;

It give back what you have given.

A Special Request

A primary school teacher asked her students to write an essay about what they would like God to do for them. At the end of the day, while marking the essays, she read one that made her very emotional. Her husband, who had just walked in, saw her crying. He asked her: "What happened?" She answered, "Read this. It is one of my student's essay."

'Oh God, tonight I ask you something very special. Make me into a television. I want to take its place and live like the TV in my house. Have my own special place, and have my family around me. To be taken seriously when I talk, I want to be the centre of attention and be heard without interruptions or questions. I want to receive the same special care that the TV receives. Have the company of my dad when he arrives home from work, even when he is tired. And I want my mom to want me when she is sad and upset, instead of ignoring me. I want to feel that my family just leaves everything aside, every now and then, just to spend some time with me. And last but not the least, please ensure that I can make them all happy and entertain them. Lord, I don't ask you for much, I just want to live like a TV.

At that moment the husband said: "My God, poor kid. What horrible parents."

The wife looked up at him and said: "That essay is our son's!"

> *Happiness is like a butterfly, which, when pursued, is always beyond our grasp, but, which, if you will sit down quietly, may alight upon you.*

Food for Thought

Imagine yourself in the line of a buffet in a luxurious restaurant, where instead of dishes of food, there are dishes of thoughts. You get to choose any and all the thoughts you wish. These thoughts will create your future experiences.

Now, if you choose thoughts that will create problems and pain, that's rather foolish. It's like choosing food that always makes you ill. It's the same with thoughts. Let us stay away from thoughts that create problems and pain.

What are you thinking right now!

Watch your thoughts, they become your words.

Watch your words, they become your actions.

Watch your actions, they become your habits.

Watch your habits, they become your character.

Watch your character, it becomes your destiny.

*   *   *

I keep six honest serving men
  They taught me all I knew;
Their names are **What** *and* **Where** *and* **When**
  And **How** *and* **Why** *and* **Who**.

—Rudyard Kipling

Christmas Present

A young priest was asked to reopen a church in suburban Brooklyn. When he saw the church, it was very run down and needed much work. He set a goal to have everything done in time to have the first service on Christmas Eve.

He worked hard, repairing benches, plastering walls, painting, etc. and on December 18 was ahead of schedule and just about finished. On December 19 a terrible rainstorm hit the area and lasted for two days.

On the 21st, the priest went over to the church. His heart sank when he saw that the roof had leaked, causing a large area of plaster fall off the front wall of the sanctuary just behind the pulpit, beginning about head high.

The priest cleaned up the mess on the floor, and not knowing what else to do but postpone the Christmas Eve service, headed home. Just outside, he noticed a flea market type sale, so he stopped. One of the items was a beautiful handmade ivory colored crocheted tablecloth with exquisite work, fine colors and cross-embroidered. It was just the right size to cover up the hole in the front wall. He bought it and headed back to the church. By this time it had started to snow. An older woman running from the opposite direction was trying to catch the bus. She missed it. The priest invited her to wait in the warm church for the next bus.

She sat on a bench and paid no attention to the priest while he got a ladder, hangers, etc. to put up the tablecloth as a wall tapestry. The priest could hardly believe how beautiful it looked and it covered up the entire problem area. Then he noticed the woman walking down the center aisle. Her face was like a sheet. "Father," she asked, "where did you get that tablecloth?"

The priest explained. The woman asked him to check the lower right corner to see if the initials, EBG were crocheted into it there. They were. These were the initials of the woman, and she had made this tablecloth 35 years ago, in Austria. The woman could hardly believe it as the priest told how he had just gotten the tablecloth. The woman explained that before the war she and her husband were well-to-do people in Austria. When the Nazis came, she was forced to leave. Her husband was going to follow her the next week. He was captured, sent to prison and never saw her husband or her home again.

The priest wanted to give her the tablecloth; but she made the priest keep it for the church. The priest insisted on driving her home, that was the least he could do.

What a wonderful service they had on Christmas eve. The church was almost full. The music and the spirit were great. At the end of the service, the priest greeted everyone at the door. One older man continued to sit in one of the pews and stare, and the priest wondered why he wasn't leaving. The man asked him where he got the tablecloth on the front wall because it was identical to one that his wife had made years ago when they lived in Austria before the war and how could there be two tablecloths so much alike.

He told the priest how the Nazis came, how he forced his wife to flee for her safety and he was supposed to follow her, but he was arrested and put in a prison. He never saw his wife or his home again all the 35 years in between.

The priest asked him if he would allow him to take him for a little ride. They drove to the same house where the priest had taken the woman three days earlier. He helped the man climb the stairs to the woman's apartment, knocked on the door and he saw the greatest Christmas reunion he could ever imagine.

The Rope

There was a mountaineer, who wanted to climb the highest mountain. He began his adventure after many years of preparation, but since he wanted the glory just for himself, he decided to climb the mountain alone.

The night felt heavy in the heights of the mountain, and the man could not see anything. All was black. Zero visibility, and the moon and the stars were covered by the clouds.

As he was climbing, only a few feet away from the top of the mountain, he slipped and fell into the air, falling at a great speed. The climber could only see black spots as he went down, and the terrible sensation of being sucked by gravity. He kept falling, and in those moments of great fear, came to his mind all the good and bad episodes of his life.

He was thinking now about how close death was getting, when all of a sudden he felt the rope tied to his waist pull him very hard.

His body was hanging in the air. Only the rope was holding him, and in that moment of stillness he had no other choice but to scream: "Help me God!"

All of a sudden, a deep voice coming from the sky replied: "What do you want me to do?"

"Save me God!"

"Do you really think I can save you?"

"Of course I believe you can."

"Then cut the rope tied to your waist."

There was a moment of silence; and then the man decided to hold on to the rope with all his strength.

The rescue team tells, that the next day a climber was found dead and frozen, his body hanging from a rope. His hands holding tight to it, only 6 feet away from the ground.

And you? How attached are you to your rope? Will you let go?

> *Often when we lose hope and think this is the end, GOD smiles from above and says, "Relax sweetheart, it's just a bend, not the end!*
>
> *   *   *
>
> *Never feel bad if people remember you only at the time of their need. Feel privileged that they think of you like a candle in the darkness of their life.*
>
> *   *   *
>
> *The first time I was in Sweden, one of my colleagues picked me up at the hotel every morning. It was September, bit cold and snowy. We would arrive early at the company and he would park far away from the entrance.*
>
> *The first day, I didn't say anything, neither the second or third day. One morning I asked him, "Do you have a fixed parking space? I've noticed we park far from the entrance even when there are no other cars in the lot."*
>
> *To which he replied, "Since we're here early we'll have time to walk. Don't you think that whoever gets in late will need a place closer to the door?" Imagine my face!*

Don't Dance so Fast

Have you ever watched kids on a merry-go-round
Or listened to the rain slapping on the ground?
Ever followed a butterfly's erratic flight
Or gazed at the sun into the fading night?

You better slow down
Don't dance so fast.
Time is short
The music won't last.

Do you run through each day on the fly.
When you ask, "How are you?"
Do you hear the reply.
When the day is done, do you lie in your bed,
with the next hundred chores running through your head?

You'd better slow down
Don't dance so fast.
Time is short
The music won't last.

Ever told your child,
We'll do it tomorrow.
And in your haste,
Not see his sorrow.

Ever lost touch,
Let a good friendship die.
Because you never had time
To call and say, 'Hi'.

You'd better slow down
Don't dance so fast.
Time is short
The music won't last.

When you run so fast to get somewhere,
You miss half the fun of getting there.
When you worry and hurry through your day,
It is like an unopened gift thrown away.

Life is not a race
Do take it slower.
Hear the music
Before the song is over.

Gautam Buddha's eight-fold path—Mr Stable

Right ...

M	-	*Meditation*
R	-	*Recollection*
S	-	*Speech*
T	-	*Thought*
A	-	*Action*
B	-	*Belief*
L	-	*Living*
E	-	*Effort*

Conditioned Minds

As a man was passing the elephants, he suddenly stopped, confused by the fact that these huge creatures were being held by only a small rope tied to their front leg. No chains, no cages. It was obvious that the elephants could, at anytime break away from their bonds but for some reason, they did not.

He saw a trainer nearby and asked why these animals just stood there and made no attempt to get away. "Well," trainer said, "when they were very young and much smaller we use the same size rope to tie them and, at that age, it's enough to hold them. As they grew up, they got conditioned to believe they cannot break away. They believe the rope can still hold them, so they never try to break free."

The man was amazed. These animals could at any time break free from their bonds but because they believed they couldn't, they were stuck right where they were.

Like the elephants, how many of us go through life hanging onto a belief that we cannot do something, simply because we failed at it once before?

Once a wise man asked God, "What is the meaning of Life?"

God replied, "Life itself has no meaning. Life is an opportunity to create a meaning."

The Great Train Journey

Life is like a journey on a train...

with its stations...

with changes of routes...

and with accidents!

We board this train when we are born and our parents are the ones who get our ticket.

We believe they will always travel on this train with us.

However, at some station our parents will get off the train, leaving us alone on this journey.

As time goes by, other passengers will board the train, many of whom will be significant—our siblings, friends, children, and even the love of our life.

Many will get off during the journey and leave a permanent vacuum in our lives.

Many will go so unnoticed that we won't even know when they vacated their seats and got off the train!

This train ride will be full of joy, sorrow, fantasy, expectations, hellos, good-byes, and farewells.

A good journey is helping, loving, having a good relationship with all co passengers...

and making sure that we give our best to make their journey comfortable.

The mystery of this fabulous journey is—

We do not know at which station we ourselves are going to get off.

So, we must live in the best way—adjust, forget, forgive, and offer the best of what we have.

It is important to do this because when the time comes for us to leave our seat... we should leave behind beautiful memories for those who will continue to travel on the train of life.

Have a very pleasant journey of life.........!

Never blame a day in your life.
Good day gives happiness.
Bad day gives experience.

*   *   *

Let's Develop 5 habits:

Mind, which never Minds.

Heart, which never Hurts.

Brain, which never Drains

Touch, which never Pains

and

Relation, which never Ends.

What is Mine

A man died. When he realized it, he saw God coming closer with a suitcase in his hand.

God: Alright son, it's time to go.

Man: So soon? I had a lot of plans.

God: I am sorry, but it's time to go.

Man: What do you have in that suitcase?

God: Your belongings.

Man: My belongings? You mean my things... clothes... money...

God: Those things were never yours, they belong to the Earth.

Man: Is it my memories?

God: No. They belong to Time.

Man: Is it my friends and family?

God: No son. They belong to the Path you travelled.

Man: Is it my wife and children?

God: No. they belong to your Heart.

Man: Then it must be my body.

God: No, no. It belongs to Dust.

Man: Then surely it must be my Soul!

God: You are sadly mistaken son. Your Soul belongs to me.

Man with tears in his eyes and full of fear took the suitcase from the God's hand and opened it. It was empty.

With heartbroken and tears down his cheek he asks God...

Man: I never owned anything?

God: That's Right. You never owned anything.

Man: Then? What was mine?

God: Your MOMENTS. Every moment you lived was yours.

Old Age Home

After his father's death, son left his mother in an old age home. He kept on visiting her on and off. After several years, he received a call from the old age home that his mother was very serious. The son immediately rushed there and found his mother to be critical, about to die. He asked his mother if he could do anything for her. The mother replied, "Please install fans in the old age home, as there are none."

Son was surprised. He questioned his mother, "All this while you were here, you never complained. Now you have only a few hours left and you are asking me to get the fans installed. Why?"

Mother replied, "It is okay. I have managed with the heat. But when your children will send you here, I am afraid, you will not be able to manage."

Do all the good you can

By all the means you can

In all the ways you can

In all the places you can

At all the times you can

To all the people you can

As long as ever you can.

Who is Happy

A crow used to live in a forest and was absolutely satisfied in life. But one day he saw a swan. "This swan is so white," he thought, "and I am so black. This swan must be the happiest bird in the world."

He expressed his thoughts to the swan. "Actually," the swan replied, "I used to feel that I was the happiest bird around until I saw a parrot, which has two colors. I now think the parrot is the happiest bird in creation."

The crow then approached the parrot. The parrot explained, "I lived a very happy life—until I saw a peacock. I have only two colors, but the peacock has multiple colors."

The crow then visited a peacock in the zoo and saw that hundreds of people had gathered to see him. After the people had left, the crow approached the peacock. "Dear peacock," the crow said, "you are so beautiful. Every day thousands of people come to see you. When people see me, they immediately shoo me away. I think you are the happiest bird on the planet."

The peacock replied, "I always thought that I was the most beautiful and happy bird on the planet. But because of my beauty, I am entrapped in this zoo. I have examined the zoo very carefully, and I have realized that crow is the only bird not kept in a cage. So for past few days I have been thinking that if I were a crow, I could happily roam everywhere."

P.S: That's our problem too. We make unnecessary comparisons with others and become sad. We don't value what God has given to us. In our own way, we all are supreme creations of the Almighty.

The Two Falcons

Once there was a king who received a gift of two magnificent falcons from Arabia. They were the most beautiful birds he had ever seen. He gave the precious birds to his head falconer to be trained.

Months passed and one day the head falconer informed the king that though one of the falcons was flying majestically, soaring high in the sky, the other bird had not moved from its branch since the day it had arrived.

The king summoned healers and sorcerers from all the land to tend to the falcon, but no one could make the bird fly. Having tried everything else, the king thought to himself, "May be I need someone more familiar with the countryside to understand the nature of this problem." So he instructed his court to get a farmer.

In the morning, the king was thrilled to see the falcon soaring high above the palace gardens. He asked the farmer, "How did you make the falcon fly?"

With head bowed, the farmer said to the king, "It was very easy, your highness. I simply cut the branch of the tree where the bird was sitting."

Moral: We are all made to fly to realize our incredible potential as human beings. But instead of doing that, we sit on our branches, clinging to the things that are familiar to us. The possibilities are endless, but for most of us, they remain undiscovered. We conform to the familiar, the comfortable, and the mundane. So for the most part, our lives are mediocre instead of exciting, thrilling and fulfilling. So let us learn to destroy the branch of fear we cling to and free ourselves to the glory of flight!

If God should Go on Strike

How good it is that God above
has never gone on strike,
because He was not treated fair
in things He didn't like.

If only once He'd given up and said,
"That's it, I'm through!
I've had enough of those on earth,
so this is what I'll do;
I'll give my orders to the sun—
cut off the heat supply!
Then just to make things really tough
and put the pressure on,
turn off the vital oxygen, till every breath is gone!"

You know, He would be justified,
if fairness was the game.
For no one has been more abused
or met with more disdain.
And yet He carries on, supplying you and me,
with all the favour of His grace, and everything for free.

Men say they want a better deal,
and so on strike they go.
But what a deal we've given God
to whom all things we owe.
We don't care whom we hurt
to gain the things we like,
but what a mess we'd all be in,
If God should go on strike!

Daughter

On the first day of their marriage, wife and husband agreed not to open the door for any visitor!

That same day, the husband's parents came to see them, and knocked on the door. Husband and the wife looked at each other... the husband wanted to open the door, but since they had an agreement, he did not, so his parents left.

After a while, the same day, the wife's parents came visiting. Wife and husband looked at each other, and even though they had an agreement, the wife with tears in her eyes whispered, "I can't do this to my parents", and she opened the door! Husband did not say anything.

Years passed and they had two boys. Afterwards, they had a third child which was a girl. The father planned a big and lavish party for the new born baby girl, and he invited everyone over.

Later that night, his wife asked him what was the reason for such a big celebration for this baby, while they did not do so for the boys!

The husband simply replied, "because she is the one who will open the door for me!"

Love is the only flower that grows and blossoms without the aid of seasons.

—Khalil Gibran

www.ingramcontent.com/pod-product-compliance
Lightning Source LLC
Chambersburg PA
CBHW071121090426
42736CB00012B/1973